Scriptural Principles For Financial Success

It's not about money, it's about God

By Dr. Kurt Grosser

Abundant Freedom Ministries

Abundant Freedom Press
Aurora, Colorado

G & G Publishing, Inc.
Abundant Freedom Press
P.O. Box 461316
Aurora, CO 80046 USA
Website: www.AbundantFreedomMinistries.com

Revised Edtion © 2007, G&G Publishing, Inc.

Scriptural Principles for Financial Success

ISBN 13: 978-09776765-0-7
ISBN 10: 0-9776765-0-1

Cover design by Archer Ellison, Inc.
Interior design and editing by Cynthia Arbuckle

Printed in the United States of America
Please visit our website for other titles and contact information:
www.AbundantFreedomMinistries.com

Dedication

This book is dedicated to all who are striving to live in financial freedom. Freedom from the bondage of the financial limitations imposed by our economic system. Freedom to live the abundant life and in the prosperity promised in the Word of God.

2 Corinthians 3:17 (NASB)
Now the Lord is the Spirit; and where the Spirit of the Lord is, there is liberty.

Acknowledgements

Special thanks to Kathy, my wife, and our children for their patience, understanding and endless encouragement.

Contents

Abundant Freedom Ministries

Chapter 1: Introduction and Overview

In This Chapter

- Why look to the Bible for financial answers?
- Mixed-up life priorities
- Correct life priorities
- Mixed-up financial priorities
- Correct financial priorities

Why should we read the Bible to learn about finances? We should read the Bible because it contains in excess of 2,300 references to economic principles, as well as guidelines on how to manage a household or a business. This book, the Bible, is a blueprint for sound economic activities. These Scriptural principles for finance were written thousands of years ago and are still active and perfectly applicable today. We will examine a large number of these principles throughout this book.

The problems in the world today are so complex and confusing that each of us must realize that Jesus is the only answer for the world. There is no other answer because what is before us is a confrontation between light and darkness, good and evil. The rich get greedier, and do not seem to be able to hang on to their possessions as the circumstances surrounding them are changing and are seemingly out of control. Often the poor feel rejected and begin to steal or even kill to get past their current problems or just to be able to eat. A chain reaction of loan defaults is just beginning and will be felt for months or even years to come. The unemployed are given little hope, and for those who are working, the fear of losing their jobs in the next round of cutbacks is mounting.

People who are in business for themselves are feeling the pressures from their bankers because of overextended credit and soon to be higher interest rates. Amounts due from others, such as accounts receivable, are being collected at an ever-slowing rate. People who depend on others to pay their bills on time so they can meet their own obligations, find themselves frustrated, seemingly hopeless, and only a breath away from bankruptcy. These problems, and numerous others, face each of us daily—and there is little hope for improvement. However, if you know the Lord Jesus Christ and trust Him, there is nothing to worry about. He is our answer because He set us free when He gave His life for us.

As believers we have to choose. We may yield to God by faith and enjoy abundant life, or we may yield to sin and endure the defeated life. God wants us to know the power of a yielded life; it will lift us above circumstances that keep us from abundant living. The abundant life begins when we yield to Him, allowing Him to live His life through us by faith.

To have faith is to believe God's Word. Not to believe is equivalent to calling God's Word not true. God cannot be separated from His word. That means if we do not believe His Word, we are calling Him a liar. The fact is that we have been saved and have been justified by Christ through faith.

It's one thing for us to believe we have eternal life by faith. It's yet another thing to have or experience abundant life by faith. To live abundantly is to serve God and not the things of this world. It seems easier for us to say that we live in Christ, than for Christ to live His life through us. For Christ to live through us requires us to have faith in Him.

We are right in the midst of a spiritual battle that is extremely crucial. We must choose between God and possessions. This is the dilemma confronting each one on this earth today. We cannot have a split commitment—meaning that we go to church on Sunday, we do know the Lord, we are saved and Spirit-filled, yet, when it comes to money or possessions, we ignore God's Word. Then we find excuses to justify in our minds why what we do is right.

We need to pray that God will open our eyes and let us see through the eyes of Christ that this is a spiritual battle between us and Satan. We allowed him to blind us from the reality that the battle was already won when Jesus died at the cross. It's over, and the victory is ours.

We spend the majority of our time thinking and worrying about our assets, material possessions, or worrying about our liabilities, things that we owe and how we might pay for them. We need income to meet our expenses, such as living costs, which can be heavy burdens. If we can agree that most of our time is spent focusing on assets, liabilities, income and expenses, then we must realize that we are part-time Christians. We believe in Jesus Christ and that He is our Lord and Savior, yet we choose to walk in the darkness of the world.

Can you see that it is our choice? We must choose, and for many of us the choice has been to sit on a fence post and jump to whichever side—depending on where things seem more favorable. It is clear that we must choose between God and mammon, meaning money and all material things.

How can God keep His promise that He will conform us to the image of His Son, when we choose to serve idols, such as money, instead of Him?

God loves us so much and He sees that we have chosen money as our idol. However, His love for us is so great and unconditional that He will never forsake us. As long as we choose to walk in darkness we are led by darkness; in other words, we are walking in the flesh. We have to walk by the Spirit, which is light.

The Bible tells us that we cannot operate in the flesh and reap the benefits of the Spirit. Many have been operating in the flesh when it comes to money or finances. Now they are reaping the consequences of the flesh. This problem is so real that many churches have subjected themselves to the yoke of slavery by believing that the multitudes and their money are their source. It is disheartening to think of the churches and ministries who are failing to see that God is their source. They have set up for themselves here on earth idols and financial empires. They are preaching and teaching God's Word, but in reality their faith is in the security of the cash flow, or in their partners, and not in God at all. Let us not be dismayed, but remember God's love is unconditional and He forgives. It is time for mankind to repent and ask God for forgiveness. The world does not know forgiveness, but God does. We cannot operate in the flesh and reap the benefits of the Spirit.

Why look to the Bible for financial answers?

John 1:1 (NIV)

[1]In the beginning was the Word, and the Word was with God, and the Word was God.

Psalm 119:105 (NIV)

[105]Your word is a lamp to my feet. And a light to my path.

There is powerful imagery in Psalm 119:105.
What does it mean to you?

____

____

____

____

____

____

____

Psalm 119:160 (NKJV)

[160]The entirety of Your word is truth, And every one of Your righteous judgments endures forever.

Deuteronomy 30:14 (NKJV)

[14]But the word is very near you, in your mouth and in your heart, that you may do it.

Matthew 6:10 (NKJV)

[10]Your kingdom come Your will be done On earth as it is in heaven.

Why did God write His Word on our hearts?

Why did Jesus tell us to pray God's will be done?

Isaiah 59:21 (NKJV)

21 "As for Me," says the LORD, "this is My covenant with them: My Spirit who is upon you, and My words which I have put in your mouth, shall not depart from your mouth, nor from the mouth of your descendants, nor from the mouth of your descendants' descendants," says the LORD, "from this time and forevermore."

What responsibility do parents have in instructing their children about God's will for finances?

____

____

____

____

____

____

____

Memorize this verse:

Romans 12:2 (NKJV)

2 And do not be conformed to this world, but be transformed by the renewing of your mind, that you may prove what is that good and acceptable and perfect will of God.

1Thessalonians 2:13 (NKJV)

13 For this reason we also thank God without ceasing, because when you received the word of God which you heard from us, you welcomed it not as the word of men, but as it is in truth, the word of God, which also effectively works in you who believe.

Hebrews 8:10 (NKJV) See also Jeremiah 31:33 (NKJV)

10 For this is the covenant that I will make with the house of Israel after those days, says the LORD: I will put My laws in their mind and write them on their hearts; and I will be their God, and they shall be My people.

How is the Word of God applicable to your life today?

____

____

____

____

____

____

____

Matthew 6:33 (NKJV)

"But seek first the kingdom of God and His righteousness, and all these things shall be added to you." (Matthew 6:33).

"When we look at these words of Jesus, we immediately find them to be the most revolutionary that human ears have ever heard. '... seek first the kingdom of God...' Even the most spiritually-minded of us argue the exact opposite, saying, 'But I *must* live; I *must* make a certain amount of money; I *must* be clothed; I *must* be fed.' The great concern of our lives is not the kingdom of God but how we are going to take care of ourselves to live. Jesus reversed the order by telling us to get the right relationship with God first, maintaining it as the primary concern of our lives, and never to place our concern on taking care of the other things of life."

(Oswald Chambers—*My Utmost for His Highest*)

A renewed mindset

God can set your priorities straight and give you a new mindset!

Mixed-up life priorities

MIXED UP LIFE PRIORITIES

1. Work
2. Finances
3. Spouse
4. Children
5. God

Life is difficult. Oftentimes the pressures of life mandate what is important and what is not. Over time, our life priorities get mixed up. Work and the resulting financial rewards take over at the sacrifice of family relationships and our relationship with God. The consequence is seen all around us in a world where divorce is common and broken families are the norm.

God will help you change. But you must ask for His help. When you do, He will begin to work in your life in an extraordinary way! These priorities are important to the God of the universe. Are they important to you?

Correct life priorities

CORRECT LIFE PRIORITIES

1. God
2. Spouse
3. Children
4. Work
5. Finances

God put our life priorities into a divine order. We must value, as our number one priority in life, a personal relationship with God. In God's eyes, our family relationships are supremely important as well, and they must be important to us. When our relationships with God and family are healthy and strong, we will have more willingness to work hard. Finances are the fruit of our labor.

What gets in the way of this divine order? Everything! Life!

It is of utmost importance that a clear and honest self-assessment of our priorities occurs on a regular basis (*at least once a month*).

Matthew 6:33 (NASB)

"But seek first His kingdom and His righteousness, and all these things will be added to you."

Mixed-up financial priorities

MIXED-UP FINANCIAL PRIORITIES

- Example:
  a. Debt
  b. Investing
  c. Needs
  d. Taxes
  e. God

The pressures of debt can be frightening. It can feel like you are drowning or carrying a heavy weight on your back. People often look to risky investments to *bail themselves out*. However, investments that promise high returns also carry the highest risk. Consequently, needs are neglected, taxes are not paid, and there is little or nothing left over for a tithe to God.

The Bible tells us that misaligned financial priorities result in a *curse*. It begins to make sense when we open our eyes and see that we have become a slave to money.

List your own financial priorities:

1. ____________________

2. ____________________

3. ____________________

4. ____________________

5. ____________________

Correct financial priorities

CORRECT FINANCIAL PRIORITIES

- Finances:
  a. God – Tithe
  b. Taxes
  c. Needs
  d. Surplus
     1. Debt
     2. Savings & Investing

God's Word provides us with a divine order to manage our money. When we put Him first by offering a tithe, and then pay our taxes and meet the needs of our household, we will be blessed. The key is to define and understand exactly what our needs are, and then apply the surplus to debt first and later to savings and investing.

The Bible also tells us that when our financial priorities are in line with His Word, we are set free. When we are set free from bondage to money, we will begin to see His blessings overflow.

How are the correct financial priorities contrary to the way of the world?

____

____

____

____

____

____

Never enough?

"NO MATTER HOW MUCH MONEY WE MAKE,
IT NEVER SEEMS TO BE ENOUGH"

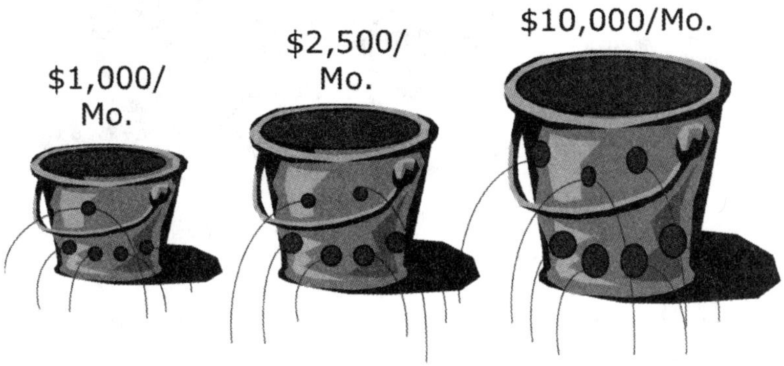

Many think, "If I had more money—that would be the answer." Those who think this way set goals to be rich. The problem is no matter how much money we make, *it will never* seem to be enough. Our spending habits will be carried with us no matter how much we make. *If you have holes in your bucket, does it matter how large the bucket is?*

What are the leaks in your financial bucket?

THE REASON FOR NEVER HAVING ENOUGH IS THAT WE FOCUS ON THE "IN" INSTEAD OF THE "OUT"

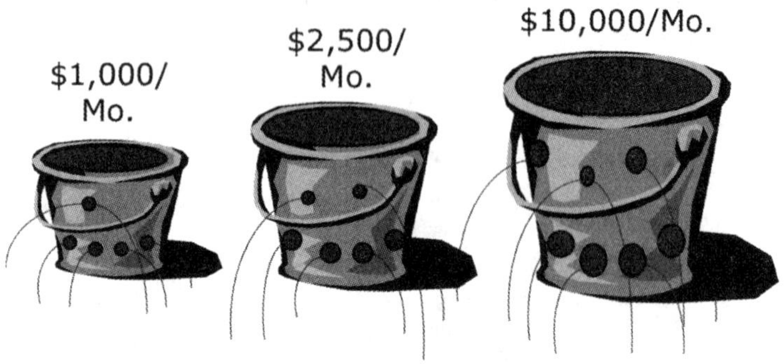

The reason for never having enough is that our focus is on the money we are making. Instead, we must focus on *how we spend what we have.* In other words, don't focus on the "IN"—or how to make more, but rather focus on the "OUT"—or where our money is being spent.

Most people focus on how much money they make. Why is it easier to focus on the "IN"?

God is in Charge of the "IN"

$1,000/Mo. $2,500/Mo. $10,000/Mo.

God's Word tells us that He will supply all of our needs (Phil. 4:19). It is He who is in charge of our "IN". It also says that he who is faithful with a little, to him more shall be given (Luke 16:10). God expects us to be good and faithful stewards of that which He has entrusted to us.

Why should you trust God with your income?
Is it really yours?

____

____

____

____

____

____

We are in Charge of the "OUT"

$1,000/Mo. $2,500/Mo. $10,000/Mo.

We are responsible for how we spend our finances. If we manage faithfully what we have, it is He who will give us more to manage. We must learn God's principles for money management (stewardship).

What ideas do you have about managing your money more effectively?

Turning it over to God

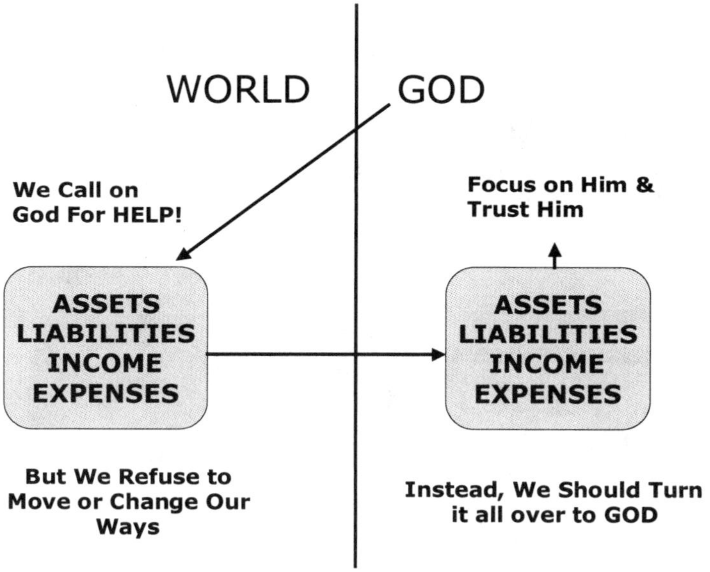

It is easy to get caught up in the financial issues of day-to-day living. When problems arise, we call on God to help us in our desperation. As soon as the storm is over, we forget Him until the next storm looms on the horizon. The problem is that we refuse to change our ways. Instead, we must turn it all over to God and focus on Him, and trust Him to guide us. We will begin to learn that He alone can get us through the storms of life.

Why is it hard to turn it *all* over to God?

____

____

____

____

____

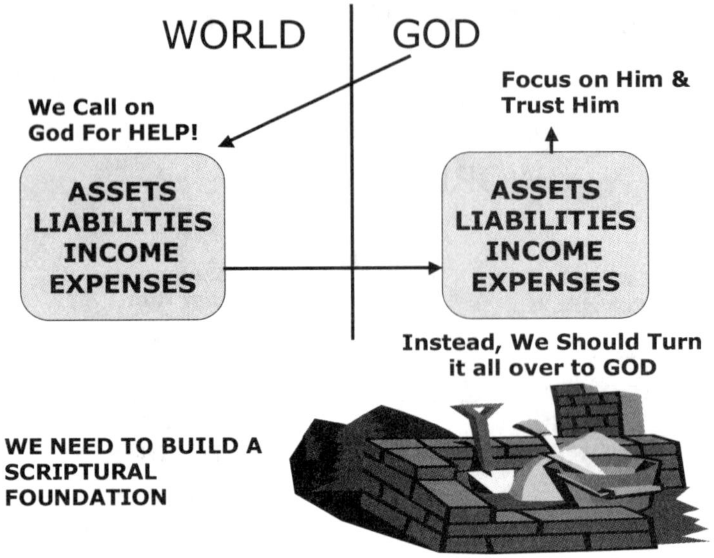

A scriptural foundation is required if we are ever to remain focused on Him and trust in His strength. There are over 2,300 scriptures dealing with finances, and they help us to build a solid foundation. Building trust is not easy. Trust is unwavering faith. Faith comes by hearing the Word of God. No shortcuts here! We have to read and hear the scriptures over and over to build our trust in Him. Financial freedom and abundance will follow.

How can you build a scriptural foundation?

____

____

____

____

____

____

____

GOD

**We Cannot At the
Same Time Focus on
GOD & Our Problem**

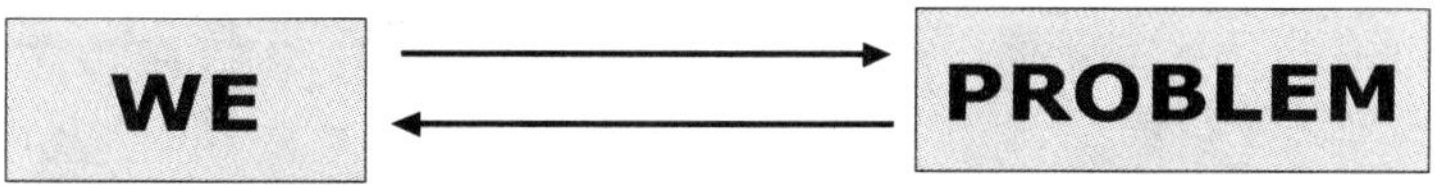

IF WE FOCUS ON OUR FINANCIAL PROBLEMS, THEY WILL IN TURN CONSUME US

While we focus on a problem we tend to worry so much about it that we forget to focus on God.

What problems have consumed you in the past?

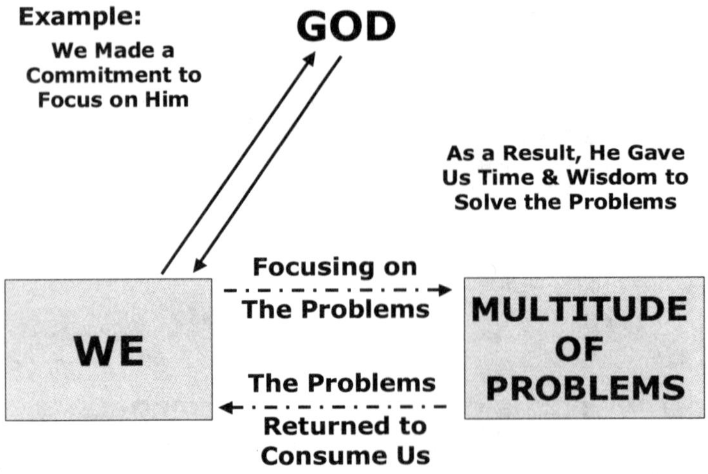

When we focus on God instead and release our problem to Him through prayer, He gives us wisdom and understanding to solve the problem.

Describe what it looks like when you focus on Him?

____

____

____

____

____

____

____

____

____

____

____

____

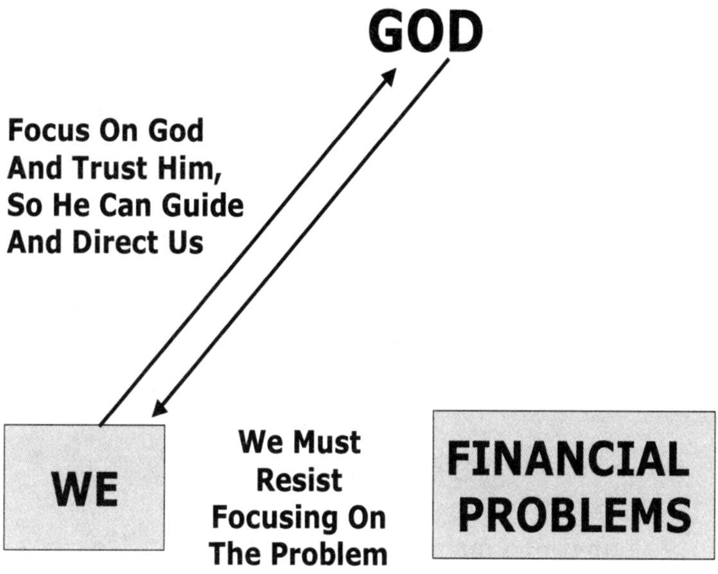

Focus on God. Look for scriptures that talk about similar problems and solutions. God will guide and direct us in solving the problems.

In the Old Testament, the people were reminded to remember how God had helped them through difficulty.

How has God helped you in the past?

____

____

____

____

____

____

____

____

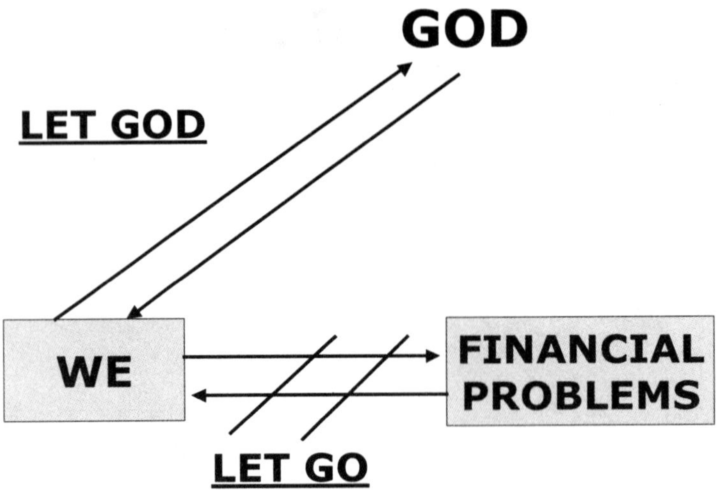

Let go of your problems and let God help you. Seek His Word for answers. God and His Word are the same—they cannot be separated.

How does it feel to let go of a problem and let God deal with it?

___

___

___

___

___

___

___

___

___

___

___

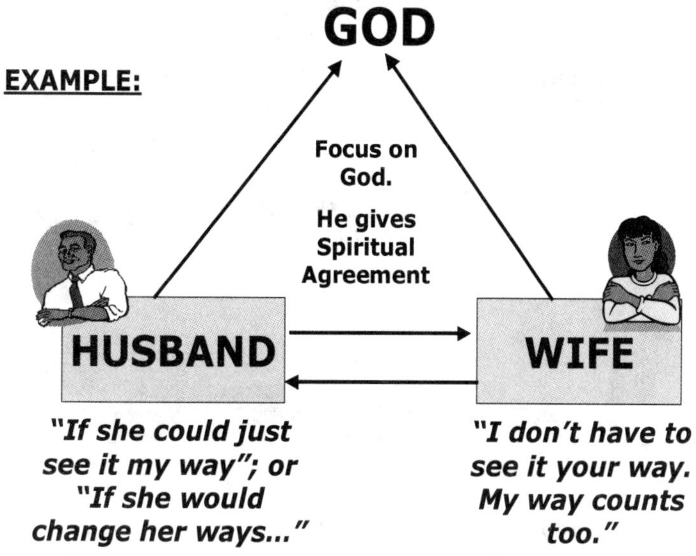

When a husband and wife have a disagreement and point the finger at each other, God cannot help. But when they focus on Him, He can help them and guide them to the solution.

In many marriages today, money is a topic that is off limits. Why is it important to write a budget together?

____

____

____

____

____

____

____

____

____

____

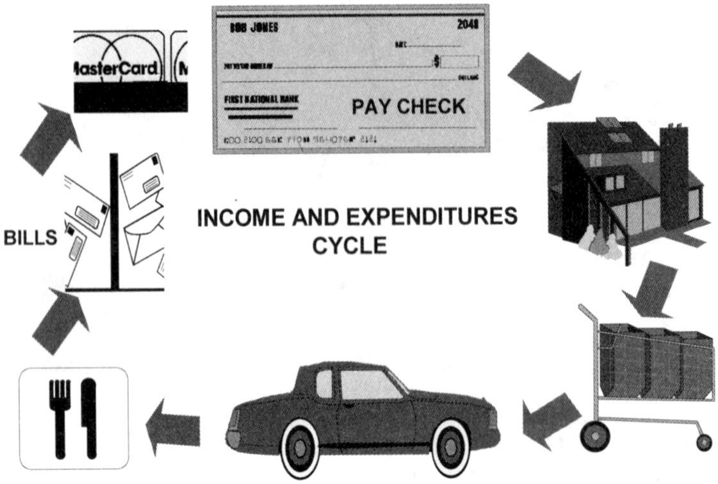

The Typical Income and Expenditures Cycle above shows that many people use their credit cards to close the gap from paycheck to paycheck. This routine becomes like a treadmill with little hope of ever getting off. However, God's Word promises other options and hope.

Why is it so hard to get out of this cycle?

___

___

___

___

___

___

___

___

___

___

___

Chapter synthesis

Take the time before the next lesson to meditate on some questions:

- What do you hope to learn from this book?
- What are the financial problems that you can already identify in your life? What solutions do you foresee?
- God wants to have the reins in all aspects of your life, including your finances. Are you ready to give Him the reins?
- What stands in your way of enjoying financial freedom?
- How often do you use your budget?
- Are there any topics or chapters that make you uneasy?

Notes and reflections...

___

___

___

___

___

___

___

___

___

___

___

Chapter 2: God's Will for Finances

In This Chapter

- How will I know His will?
- Abraham's blessing
- Where faith comes from
- Three action steps to take

Have you ever wondered what the will of God is? When we ask God to reveal His will to us, we realize that God's will is His Word, the Bible. His Words need to abide in us so that we *know* God's will, which enables us to *do* His will.

God wants us to *learn* His will. His will is good, acceptable and perfect. We need to seek the will of God so that we can *learn to know* His ways. The scriptures tell us to "Seek, and you shall find," and "Ask and you shall receive." We have to take action by getting into the Word and doing our part and God will do the rest.

God's Word is already in our heart (our spirit) according to the scriptures, but we must take action to continually renew our minds by reading the Word and doing what it says. Scriptures tell us that God's Word (His will) is good, acceptable and perfect. When we obey the will of God we are partakers of His kingdom and His promises.

The authority of the Word is God Himself. Today and everlasting, His Word is living truth and righteousness. Only God's Word can separate our mind (soul) and spirit. As we feed on the Word of God, that is, meditate on it day and night, our spirit being, also referred to as our inner man, becomes active. Eventually our mind will yield to the direction of our spirit. But only the Word of God can accomplish this separation. As His Word says, God is able to judge even our hearts and intentions. We must, therefore, fully surrender to Him so He can teach us His ways.

We are not to rely on our own thoughts and understanding. Often our understanding is in direct opposition to the Word. We are not to worry because Jesus said that the Holy Spirit would help us to learn and understand His Word.

It is important that we hold to the Word, no matter what, and resist Satan when he tries to manipulate our thoughts and actions. It has to be God's Word (His will) within us that directs each step. We have to remember that with God all things are possible.

Eventually our mind will yield to the direction of our spirit. We must fully surrender to Him so He can teach us His ways.

In this chapter, we will examine scriptures that reveal God's will for our finances.

It is God's will that we prosper. He wants to bless everything we put our hands to.

The authority of the Word is God Himself. If we know His Word and act on it, we will be blessed in everything we do.

How will I know His will?

John 15:7-8 (NKJV)

[7]If you abide in Me, and My words abide in you, you will ask what you desire, and it shall be done for you. [8]By this My Father is glorified, that you bear much fruit; so you will be My disciples.

Joshua 1:8 (NKJV)

[8]This Book of the Law shall not depart from your mouth, but you shall meditate in it day and night, that you may observe to do according to all that is written in it. For then you will make your way prosperous, and then you will have good success.

Abide is often translated Remain.
What does it mean that God's Words remain in us?

____

____

____

____

____

____

____

According to these verses, when we do our part,
He will do His. What is our part?

____

____

____

____

____

Definition of Success:

The achievement of something desired, planned, or attempted. (*dictionary.com*)

Hebrews 10:35-36 (NKJV)

[35]Therefore do not cast away your confidence, which has great reward.

[36]For you have need of endurance, so that after you have done the will of God, you may receive the promise.

God really wants us to prosper?

Definition of Prosperous:

Having success; flourishing(*dictionary.com*)

Prosperous

3 John 1:2 (NKJV)

[2]Beloved, I pray that you may prosper in all things and be in health, just as your soul prospers.

Deuteronomy 30:9 (NKJV)

[9]The LORD your God will make you abound in all the work of your hand, in the fruit of your body, in the increase of your livestock, and in the produce of your land for good. For the LORD will again rejoice over you for good as He rejoiced over your fathers.

In Deuteronomy 30:9, God describes what He will do for His people when they return and obey Him. Using this scripture, list all that God will make you abound in.

____

____

____

The Lord rejoices over you when you obey Him.

How does that make you feel?

The Lord will again rejoice over you.

Psalm 128:1-2 (NIV)

[1]Blessed are all who fear the Lord, who walk in his ways.
[2]You will eat the fruit of your labor; blessings and prosperity will be yours.

Definition of Blessing:

To confer well-being or prosperity on. (*dictionary.com*)

Memorize this verse:

Jeremiah 29:11 (NIV)

[11]For I know the plans I have for you," declares the LORD, "plans to prosper you and not to harm you, plans to give you hope and a future."

Psalm 1:1-3 (NKJV)

[1]Blessed is the man Who walks not in the counsel of the ungodly, Nor stands in the path of sinners, Nor sits in the seat of the scornful; [2]But his delight is in the law of the LORD, And in His law he meditates day and night. [3]He shall be like a tree Planted by the rivers of water, That brings forth its fruit in its season, Whose leaf also shall not wither; And whatever he does shall prosper.

**Take the time to reflect on your own tree of life.
Where is it planted? What is its source?**

Psalm 35:27 (NKJV)

[27]Let them shout for joy and be glad, Who favor my righteous cause; And let them say continually, "Let the LORD be magnified, Who has pleasure in the prosperity of His servant."

Deuteronomy 5:32-33 (NIV)

[32]So be careful to do what the LORD your God has commanded you; do not turn aside to the right or to the left. [33]Walk in all the ways that the LORD your God has commanded you, so that you may live and prosper and prolong your days in the land which you will possess.

Joshua 1:7-9 (NKJV)

[7]Only be strong and very courageous, that you may observe to do according to all the law which Moses My servant commanded you; do not turn from it to the right hand or to the left, that you

may prosper wherever you go. [8]This Book of the Law shall not depart from your mouth, but you shall meditate in it day and night, that you may observe to do according to all that is written in it. For then you will make your way prosperous, and then you will have good success. [9]Have I not commanded you? Be strong and of good courage; do not be afraid, nor be dismayed, for the L*ORD* *your God is with you wherever you go."*

"At first, we want the awareness of being guided by God. But then as we grow spiritually, we live so fully aware of God that we do not even need to ask what His will is, because the thought of choosing another way will never occur to us." (Oswald Chambers—*My Utmost for His Highest*)

How well do you think this statement fits the verses above concerning God's will?

____

____

____

____

____

____

____

____

Abraham's blessing is ours

Galatians 3:5-10 (The Message)

Answer this question: Does the God who lavishly provides you with his own presence, his Holy Spirit, working things in your lives you could never do for yourselves, does He do these things because of your strenuous moral striving or because you trust Him to do them in you? Don't these things happen among you just as they happened with Abraham? He believed God, and that act of belief was turned into a life that was right with God.

Is it not obvious to you that persons who put their trust in Christ (not persons who put their trust in the law!) are like Abraham: children of faith? It was all laid out beforehand in scripture that God would set things right with non-Jews by faith.

Scripture anticipated this in the promise to Abraham: "All nations will be blessed in you."

So those now who live by faith are blessed along with Abraham, who lived by faith—this is no new doctrine! And that means that anyone who tries to live by his own effort, independent of God, is doomed to failure. Scripture backs this up: "Utterly cursed is every person who fails to carry out every detail written in the Book of the Law."

Romans 4:3 (NASB)

3*For what does the scripture say, "Abraham believed God, and it was credited to him for righteousness."*

Romans 4:16-17 (NIV)

16*Therefore, the promise comes by faith, so that it may be by grace and may be guaranteed to all Abraham's offspring—not only to those who are of the law but also to those who are of the faith Abraham. He is the father of us all.*
17*As it is written: "I have made you a father of many nations." He is our father in the sight of God, in whom he believed—the God who gives life to the dead and calls things that are not as though they were.*

Using the previous three scriptures, fill in the blanks:

So those now who _______ ___ ________are blessed along with Abraham.

"Abraham ______________God and it was credited to him for righteousness." Therefore, the promise comes by ___________.

FAITH

Genesis 17:3-8 (NKJV)

3 Then Abram fell on his face, and God talked with him, saying:
4 "As for Me, behold, My covenant is with you, and you shall be
a father of many nations. 5 No longer shall your name be called
Abram, but your name shall be Abraham; for I have made you
a father of many nations. 6 I will make you exceedingly fruitful;
and I will make nations of you, and kings shall come from you.
7 And I will establish My covenant between Me and you and your
descendants after you in their generations, for an everlasting
covenant, to be God to you and your descendants after you. 8 Also
I give to you and your descendants after you the land in which
you are a stranger, all the land of Canaan, as an everlasting
possession; and I will be their God."

Above is Abraham's Blessing.
As you read it, what words speak to your heart?

____

____

____

____

____

____

____

If the promise comes by faith, where does our faith come from?

Romans 10:17 (NKJV)

17 So then faith comes by hearing, and hearing by the Word of God.

There is no shortcut. We must read and hear the Word of God in order to grow in faith, until we learn to turn to Him in everything. *Trust in God is unwavering faith. Faith is the belief in things unseen.*

Galatians 3:2 (NASB)

2 This is the only thing I want to find out from you: did you receive the Spirit by the works of the Law, or by hearing with faith?

Matthew 9:28-29 (NASB)

28 When He entered the house, the blind men came up to Him and Jesus said to them, "Do you believe that I am able to do this?" They said to Him, "Yes, Lord." 29 Then He touched their eyes saying, "It shall be done to you according to your faith."

How did two blind men know with certainty that Jesus could heal them, if they had never seen His miracles?

____

____

____

____

____

____

____

____

Matthew 17:20(b) (NKJV)

Assuredly, I say to you, if you have faith as a mustard seed, you will say to this mountain, 'Move from here to there,' and it will move; and nothing will be impossible for you.

John 4:40-42 (NKJV)

40So when the Samaritans had come to Him, they urged Him to stay with them; and He stayed there two days. 41And many more believed because of His own word.42Then they said to the woman, "Now we believe, not because of what you said, for we ourselves have heard Him and we know that this is indeed the Christ, the Savior of the world."

John 10:4(b)-5 (NKJV)

And the sheep follow Him, for they know His voice. 5Yet they will by no means follow a stranger, but will flee from him, for they do not know the voice of strangers."

Acts 7:31-32 (NKJV)

31When Moses saw it, he marveled at the sight; and as he drew near to observe, the voice of the Lord came to him, 32saying, 'I am the God of your fathers—the God of Abraham, the God of Isaac, and the God of Jacob.' And Moses trembled and dared not look.

When have you heard God's voice in the past?
What did it sound like?

____

____

____

____

____

____

____

The authority of the Word

Hebrews 4:12 (NKJV)

[2]For the word of God is living and powerful, and sharper than any two-edged sword, piercing even to the division of soul and spirit, and of joints and marrow, and is a discerner of the thoughts and intents of the heart.

Psalm 119:160 (NASB)

[160]The sum of Your word is truth, And every one of Your righteous ordinances is everlasting.

Memorize this verse:

2 Timothy 3:16-17 (NKJV)

[16]All scripture is given by inspiration of God, and is profitable for doctrine, for reproof, for correction, for instruction in righteousness, [17]that the man of God may be complete, thoroughly equipped for every good work.

Matthew 5:17-18 (NASB)

[17]"Do not think that I came to abolish the Law or the Prophets; I did not come to abolish but to fulfill. [18]For truly, I say to you, until heaven and earth pass away, not the smallest letter or stroke shall pass from the law until all is accomplished.

In the subsequent lessons we will explore some of the specific commands that God has for our finances. Based on the above scriptures, list four reasons why we should trust the authority of His Word in the area of finances.

1.____

2.____

3.____

4.____

John 14:26 (NASB)

26 But the Helper, the Holy Spirit, whom the Father will send in My name, He will teach you all things, and bring to your remembrance all things that I said to you.

Reflect on what we have learned so far—

What is the Holy Spirit beginning to say to you?

Acting on the Word

Matthew 7:7-8 (NASB)

7"Ask, and it will be given to you; seek, and you will find; knock, and it will be opened to you. 8For everyone who asks receives, and he who seeks finds, and to him who knocks it will be opened.

1 John 5:14-15 (NASB)

14 This is the confidence which we have before Him, that, if we ask anything according to His will, He hears us. 15And if we know that He hears us in whatever we ask, we know that we have the requests that we have asked from Him.

James 1:22-25 (NKJV)

22But be doers of the word, and not hearers only, deceiving yourselves. 23For if anyone is a hearer of the word and not a doer, he is like a man observing his natural face in a mirror; 24for he observes himself, goes away, and immediately forgets what kind of man he was. 25But he who looks into the perfect law of liberty and continues in it, and is not a forgetful hearer but a doer of the work, this one will be blessed in what he does.

**God wants you to be a doer of His Word.
Based on what you have learned, what would your life look like if you became a doer of His Word?**

____

____

____

____

____

____

____

____

Three action steps to take

First Step—read the Bible and meditate on it day and night.

Psalm 1:1-3 (NASB)

[1]*How blessed is the man who does not walk in the counsel of the wicked, nor stand in the path of sinners, nor sit in the seat of scoffers!* [2]*But his delight is in the law of the Lord, and in His law he meditates day and night.* [3]*He will be like a tree firmly planted by streams of water, which yields its fruit in its season, and its leaf does not wither; and in whatever he does, he prospers.*

Joshua 1:8 (NASB)

[8]*This book of the Law shall not depart from your mouth, but you shall meditate on it day and night, so that you may be careful to do according to all that is written in it; for then you will make your way prosperous, and then you will have success.*

1 Peter 2:1-3 (NASB)

[1]Therefore, putting aside all malice and all deceit and hypocrisy, and envy and all slander, [2]like newborn babies, long for the pure milk of the word, so that by it you may grow in respect to salvation, [3]if you have tasted the kindness of the Lord.

Psalm 119:105 (NASB)

[105]Your word is a lamp to my feet and a light to my path.

What will you do to take the first step?

____

____

____

____

____

____

____

____

Second Step—bridle your tongue

1 Peter 3:10 (NASB)

[10]The one who desires life, to love and see good days, must keep his tongue from evil and his lips from speaking deceit.

What you *say* is what you get.

2 Corinthians 4:13 (NASB)

[13]But having the same spirit of faith, according to what is written, "I believed, therefore I spoke," we also believe, therefore we also speak.

2 Corinthians 10:11 (NASB)

[11]Let such a person consider this, that we are in word by letters when absent, such persons we are also in deed when present.

Psalm 52:2-4 (NASB)

[2]Your tongue devises destruction, like a sharp razor, O worker of deceit. [3]You love evil more than good, falsehood more than speaking what is right. [4]You love all words that devour, O deceitful tongue.

James 3:5-6 (NASB)

[5]So also the tongue is a small part of the body, and yet it boasts of great things.

See how great a forest is set aflame by such a small fire! [6]And the tongue is a fire, the very world of iniquity; the tongue is set among our members as that which defiles the entire body, and sets on fire the course of our life, and is set on fire by hell.

James 3:8-12 (NASB)

[8]But no one can tame the tongue; it is a restless evil and full of deadly poison. [9]With it we bless our Lord and Father, and with it we curse men, who have been made in the likeness of God; [10]from the same mouth come both blessing and cursing. My brethren, these things ought not to be this way. [11]Does a fountain send out from the same opening both fresh and bitter water? [12]Can a fig tree, my brethren, produce olives, or a vine produce figs? Nor can salt water produce fresh.

Matthew 15:11 (NASB)

[11]"It is not what enters into the mouth that defiles the man, but what proceeds out of the mouth, this defiles the man."

Third step—put away the old self

World	God
Dead in transgressions and sins	Loved by God
Followers of the world and Satan	Recipients of God's mercy, grace, and kindness
Disobedient to God	Alive and raised up with Christ
Gratifiers of our sinful lusts	Saved by grace
Followers of our every desire and thought	Seated with Christ in heaven
Objects of God's wrath	God's workmanship

Colossians 3:1-10 (NASB)

1Therefore if you have been raised up with Christ, keep seeking the things above, where Christ is, seated at the right hand of God. 2Set your mind on the things above, not on the things that are on earth. 3For you have died and your life is hidden with Christ in God. 4When Christ, who is our life, is revealed, then you also will be revealed with Him in glory.

5Therefore consider the members of your earthly body as dead to immorality, impurity, passion, evil desire, and greed, which amounts to idolatry. 6For it is because of these things that the wrath of God will come upon the sons of disobedience, 7and in them you also once walked, when you were living in them. 8But now you also, put them all aside: anger, wrath, malice, slander, and abusive speech from your mouth. 9Do not lie to one another, since you laid aside the old self with its evil practices, 10and have put on the new self who is being renewed to a true knowledge according to the image of the One who created him.

Ephesians 4:22(b) (NASB)

...lay aside the old self, which is being corrupted in accordance with the lusts of deceit.

Ephesians 4:25-31 (NASB)

25Therefore, laying aside falsehood, SPEAK TRUTH EACH ONE OF YOU WITH HIS NEIGHBOR, for we are members of one another. 26BE ANGRY, AND YET DO NOT SIN; do not let the sun go down on your anger, 27and do not give the devil an opportunity. 28He who steals must steal no longer; but rather he must labor, performing with his own hands what is good, so that he will have something to share with one who has need. [29]Let no unwholesome word proceed from your mouth, but only such a word as is good for edification according to the need of the moment, so that it will give grace to those who hear. [30]Do not grieve the Holy Spirit of God, by whom you were sealed for the day of redemption. [31]Let all bitterness and wrath and anger and clamor and slander be put away from you, along with all malice.

We evaluate ourselves with God's guidance and by repentance—a change of mind—a change of heart—a change of will.

When we begin to evaluate our past, every form of reasoning, defensiveness and frustration will surface. When we examine our present position, depending on the result, we either feel defeated and discouraged, or proud and boastful of our accomplishments. God forgives our past transgressions and we cannot change anything in the past even if we wanted to. God's Word says that the old has gone and the new has come (2 Cor. 5:17). That means that through Jesus Christ we have a new beginning.

We need God's guidance in evaluating our present situation. The Lord knows our hearts and motives and attitudes better than we do. It is for that reason that we must surrender ourselves to Him for guidance and direction.

Let us search our own hearts

1 Chronicles 28:9 (NASB)

[9]"As for you, my son Solomon, know the God of your father, and serve Him with a whole heart and a willing mind; for the LORD searches all hearts, and understands every intent of the thoughts. If you seek Him, He will let you find Him; but if you forsake Him, He will reject you forever.

Psalm 139:23-24 (NASB)

[23]Search me, O God, and know my heart; Try me and know my anxious thoughts;[24]And see if there be any hurtful way in me, And lead me in the everlasting way.

Proverbs 20:27 (NASB)

[27]The spirit of man is the lamp of the LORD, Searching all the innermost parts of his being.

What is the condition of your heart right now?

____

____

____

____

____

____

____

____

Examine your old habits

Hebrews 12:15 (NASB)

[15]See to it that no one comes short of the grace of God; that no root of bitterness springing up causes trouble, and by it many be defiled.

Lamentations 3:19-21 (NASB)

[19]Remember my affliction and my wandering, the wormwood
and bitterness.[20]Surely my soul remembers And is bowed down
within me.[21]This I recall to my mind, Therefore I have hope.

We must break the spiritual bondage between us and the world

Romans 7:6 (NASB)

[6]But now we have been released from the Law, having died to that by which we were bound, so that we serve in newness of the Spirit and not in oldness of the letter.

Chapter synthesis

In this chapter we learned that it is God's will for us to prosper and to receive, or accept His blessings. The Word of God is His authority and when we act on it in faith, we will truly be blessed.

The following verses are great affirmation prayers concerning this chapter:

- Ps. 40:8
- Ps. 143:10
- Matt. 6:10
- Matt. 12:50
- Eph. 1:17-18
- Rev 4:11

Also, take some time to mediate on these verses:

- Luke 12:4-7
- Eph. 1:1-12
- Col. 1:9
- Hebrews 13:20-21

Notes and reflections…

Chapter 3: Financial Problems (Bondage)

In This Chapter

- How do I know if I am in bondage?
- The strongholds of bondage
- Prayer for deliverance

It is important to be able to detect symptoms and causes of financial problems (bondage). When we are in bondage we are virtually consumed by our problems, and therefore are ineffective in focusing on true solutions.

God's Word tells us that we should train up a child in the way he should go, even when he is old he will not depart from it. This is why it is difficult for us to give up our old and familiar ways and begin to trust God's Word and His scriptures, which are often directly opposite from what we are used to. This is a universal problem that exists among the affluent as well as among the poor.

From the following symptoms and causes, you should be able to identify financial problems you are experiencing. For example:

- Excessive credit
- Past due bills
- Overspending
- Never having enough

can be seen all around us. We have been taught over the years to buy now and pay later. To some, the use of credit cards is a way of life, and most individuals and families continue to borrow. Many people believe that if they can "squeeze in" the monthly payment, they should buy. They fail to question the cost or the need of what they are buying. The use of credit often leads to overspending, and eventually one cannot keep up with all obligations.

Other examples are:

- Worry
- Anger
- Fear

Often we worry about not having enough to meet our needs. Others, whose needs are met, want more, but never seem to get enough. Society has led us to believe that we are insignificant if we have little, and has classified us by how much we have. As a result, many of us constantly worry about what other people think of us. We then buy almost anything on credit to "buy" or gain acceptance. Worrying about bills leads to anger over the situation and over the bondage we are in. Then the fear of losing some or all possessions takes over. Other examples are:

- Greed
- Envy
- Bitterness
- Jealousy

These symptoms are the result of not being content with what one has. We are led to want more and more to keep up with our neighbors. Greed or envy often lead to bitter jealousy, ending in a competition to see who can outdo the other by buying more on credit without realizing the ultimate disaster. Other symptoms of financial bondage frequently include resentment, over-commitment to work, unethical dealings, deceitfulness, a "get-rich-quick" attitude, and little or no financial planning.

In this chapter we will look at what God's Word can tell us about our financial problems, both symptoms and causes, and how we can deal with them.

How do I know if I am in bondage?

Definition of Bondage:

The state of being bound; condition of being under restraint; restraint of personal liberty by compulsion; involuntary servitude; slavery; captivity. 2. Obligation; tie of duty. (dictionary.com)

The following list describes some of the more common *symptoms*:

Desire for worldly riches

Proverbs 28:20 (NKJV)

20 A faithful man will abound with blessings, But he who hastens to be rich will not go unpunished.

Ecclesiastes 5:10 (NKJV)

10 He who loves silver will not be satisfied with silver; Nor he who loves abundance, with increase. This also is vanity.

What are your desires?

____

____

____

____

____

____

____

Trust in worldly possessions

Psalm 62:10(b) (NKJV)

[10]If riches increase, Do not set your heart on them.

1 Timothy 6:17 (NASB)

[17]Instruct those who are rich in this present world not to be conceited or to fix their hope on the uncertainty of riches, but on God, who richly supplies us with all things to enjoy.

Jeremiah 48:7(a) (NKJV)

[7]For because you have trusted in your works and your treasures, You also shall be taken. [28]He who trusts in his riches will fall, But the righteous will flourish like the green leaf.

Proverbs 11:28 (NASB)

[28]He who trusts in his riches will fall, But the righteous will flourish like the green leaf.

Proverbs 23:4-5 (NASB)

[4]Do not weary yourself to gain wealth, Cease from your consideration of it.[5]When you set your eyes on it, it is gone. For wealth certainly makes itself wings Like an eagle that flies toward the heavens.

Luke 12:15 (NASB)

15Then He said to them, "Beware, and be on your guard against every form of greed; for not even when one has an abundance does his life consist of his possessions."

Do you trust in your possessions more than you trust God?

____

____

____

____

____

Are you trying to keep up with the Joneses?

____

____

____

____

____

____

____

____

____

____

Suggested reading:

The Love of Money (1 Timothy 6:3-20).

Further verses:

- Job 36:1
- Prov. 11:4
- Prov. 13:7
- Prov. 27:24,
- Prov. 28:19-20
- Prov. 28:22
- Prov. 21:5
- Matt. 13:22
- Mark 10:23-25

Poor planning

Luke 14:28-30 (NASB)

[28]"For which one of you, when he wants to build a tower, does not first sit down and calculate the cost to see if he has enough to complete it? [29]"Otherwise, when he has laid a foundation and is not able to finish, all who observe it begin to ridicule him, [30]saying, 'This man began to build and was not able to finish.'"

Do you really have a financial plan?

____

____

____

____

____

____

____

____

Lack of tithing

Proverbs 11:24 (NASB)

[24]There is one who scatters, and yet increases all the more, And there is one who withholds what is justly due, and yet it results only in want.

Malachi 3:8-9 (NKJV)

[8]"Will a man rob God? Yet you have robbed Me !But you say, 'In what way have we robbed You?' In tithes and offerings. [9]You are cursed with a curse, For you have robbed Me, Even this whole nation."

Laziness

Proverbs 10:4-5 (NKJV)

[4]He who has a slack hand becomes poor, But the hand of the diligent makes rich.[5]He who gathers in summer is a wise son; He who sleeps in harvest is a son who causes shame.

Proverbs 19:15(NKJV)

[15]Laziness casts one into a deep sleep, And an idle person will suffer hunger.

Proverbs 6:10-11(NKJV)

[10]A little sleep, a little slumber, A little folding of the hands to sleep—[11]So shall your poverty come on you like a prowler, And your need like an armed man.

Proverbs 6:10-11 (NKJV)

[10]A little sleep, a little slumber, A little folding of the hands to sleep—[11]So shall your poverty come on you like a prowler, And your need like an armed man.

2 Thessalonians 3:10(b) (NKJV))

If anyone will not work, neither shall he eat.

Why can you trust God to use the money you give?

No commitment to work

Proverbs 12:11 (NLT)

[11]Hard work means prosperity; only fools idle away their time.

What is your work ethic?

Over-committed to work

Psalm 39:6 (NLT)

6 We are merely moving shadows, and all our busy rushing ends in nothing. We heap up wealth for someone else to spend.

Ecclesiastes 4:8 (NLT)

8 This is the case of a man who is all alone, without a child or a brother, yet who works hard to gain as much wealth as he can. But then he asks himself, "Who am I working for? Why am I giving up so much pleasure now?" It is all so meaningless and depressing.

When does your job rule your life?

____

____

____

____

____

____

____

____

Other common symptoms:

- Overdue bills piling up
- Overspending
- Never having enough
- Little or no financial planning

Every *symptom* has a *cause*. If you have symptoms of bondage, you must look at the root cause of your financial problems.

Common causes of financial problems

Debt (credit)

Definition of Debt:

That which is due from one person to another, whether money, goods, or services; that which one person is bound to pay to another, or to perform for his benefit; thing owed; obligation; liability. 2. A duty neglected or violated; a fault; a sin; a trespass.

(*dictionary.com*)

Proverbs 22:7 (NIV)

7The rich rules over the poor, And the borrower is servant to the lender.

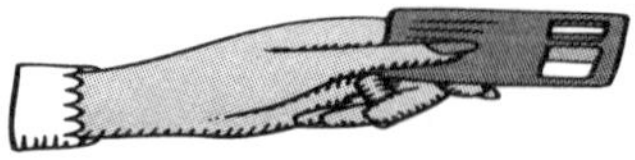

What do you think it feels like to be a servant to creditors?

____

____

____

____

____

Habakkuk 2:6-7 (NASB)

6"Will not all of these take up a taunt-song against him, Even mockery and insinuations against him.

And say, 'Woe to him who increases what is not his—
For how long—And makes himself rich with loans?'"
7"Will not your creditors rise up suddenly,

And those who collect from you awaken?

Indeed, you will become plunder for them."

Want (directly related to never having enough)

Proverbs 11:24 (NASB)

24 There is one who scatters, and yet increases all the more, And there is one who withholds what is justly due, and yet it results only in want.

How much money would it take for you to feel that you have enough?

Idolatry

1 John 5:21 (NKJV)

21 Little children, keep yourselves from idols. Amen.

1 Corinthians 10:7, 14 (NKJV)

7 And do not become idolaters as were some of them. As it is written, "The people sat down to eat and drink, and rose up to play." 14 Therefore, my beloved, flee from idolatry.

What idols do you have in your life?

Greed

Luke 12:15 (NASB)

[15]Then He said to them, "Beware, and be on your guard against every form of greed; for not even when one has an abundance does his life consist of his possessions."

Proverbs 21:26 (NASB)

[26]All day long he is craving, While the righteous gives and does not hold back.

Psalm 10:3 (NASB)

[3]For the wicked boasts of his heart's desire,
And the greedy man curses and spurns the LORD.

We all feel greed at some times.
Under what circumstances do you feel greedy?

____

____

____

____

____

____

____

Suggested reading:

The Parable of the Rich Fool (Luke 12:13-21).

Envy (don't want someone else to have it)

Proverbs 14:30 (NKJV)

[30]A sound heart is life to the body, But envy is rottenness to the bones.

Jealousy (you want to have it)

James 3:14, 16 (NKJV)

[14]But if you have bitter envy and self-seeking in your hearts, do not boast and lie against the truth. [16]For where envy and self-seeking exist, confusion and every evil thing are there.

Why do you think people feel envious or jealous about what others have?

____

____

____

____

____

____

____

____

Fear (of not having enough)

Luke 12:25-26 (NASB)

[25]"And which of you by worrying can add a single hour to his life's span?" [26]"If then you cannot do even a very little thing, why do you worry about other matters?"

Proverbs 29:25 (NKJV)

[25]The fear of man brings a snare, But whoever trusts in the LORD shall be safe.

Proverbs 10:24 (NKJV)

[24]The fear of the wicked will come upon him, And the desire of the righteous will be granted.

Romans 8:15 (NKJV)

[15]*For you did not receive the spirit of bondage again to fear, but you received the Spirit of adoption by whom we cry out, "Abba, Father."*

How much is enough?
Would you feel less fearful if you had it?

____

____

____

____

____

____

____

____

Deception

Colossians 1:13 (NASB)

[13]*For He rescued us from the domain of darkness, and transferred us to the kingdom of His beloved Son.*

Fraud (unethical dealings)

Proverbs 13:11 (NKJV)

[11]*Wealth gained by dishonesty will be diminished, But he who gathers by labor will increase.*

What qualifies, in your mind, as deceiving or unethical behavior?

Financial strongholds

In many situations, our financial problems (bondage) have become *strongholds*.

Galatians 5:1 (NASB)

1 It was for freedom that Christ set us free; therefore keep standing firm and do not be subject again to a yoke of slavery.

What is this "yoke of slavery"? Financial strongholds, like a yoke, keep us doing what we know is wrong, e.g. buying on credit.

What is the "yoke of slavery" in your life?

Romans 7:14-17 (NASB)

*[14]For we know that the Law is spiritual, but I am of flesh, sold
into bondage to sin. [15]For what I am doing, I do not understand;
for I am not practicing what I would like to do, but I am doing
the very thing I hate. [16]But if I do the very thing I do not want
to do, I agree with the Law, confessing that the Law is good.
[17]So now, no longer am I the one doing it, but sin which dwells
in me.*

Ephesians 6:12 (NASB)

[12]For our struggle is not against flesh and blood, but against the rulers, against the powers, against the world forces of this darkness, against the spiritual forces of wickedness in the heavenly places.

Financial problems (bondage) usually come in threes—to form strongholds—within us.

Ecclesiastes 4:12 (NASB)

[12]And if one can overpower him who is alone, two can resist him. A cord of three strands is not quickly torn apart.

Examples of strongholds

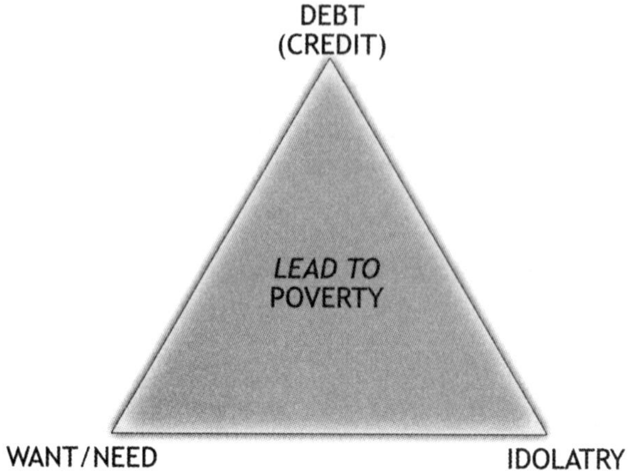

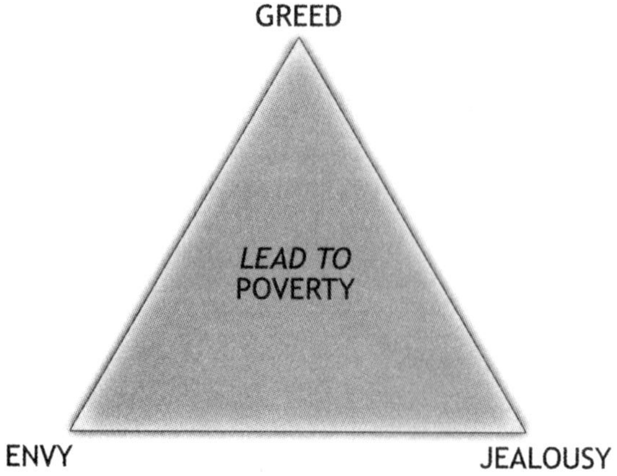

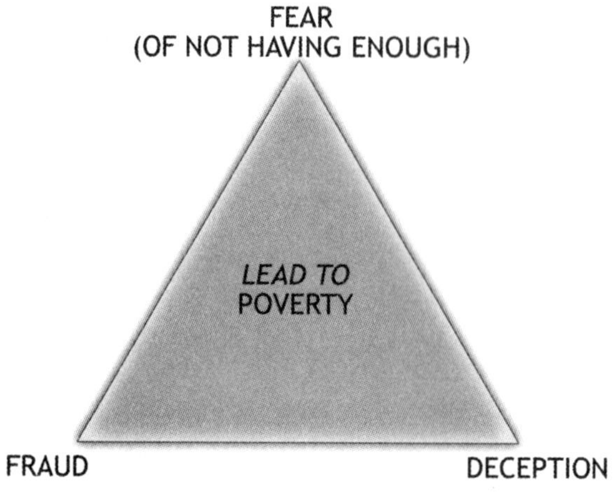

What financial strongholds exist in your life?

____

____

____

____

____

____

____

____

There is hope!

Colossians 1:13 (NKJV)

13 He has delivered us from the power of darkness and conveyed us into the kingdom of the Son of His love...

Strongholds can be broken!

2 Corinthians 10:3-5 (NASB)

*3 For though we walk in the flesh, we do not war according to
the flesh, 4 for the weapons of our warfare are not of the flesh,
but divinely powerful for the destruction of fortresses. 5 We are
destroying speculations and every lofty thing raised up against
the knowledge of God, and we are taking every thought captive
to the obedience of Christ.*

Psalm 2:3 (NKJV)

3 "Let us break Their bonds in pieces And cast away Their cords from us."

Jeremiah 5:5(b) (NASB)

But they too, with one accord, have broken the yoke and burst the bonds.

Why can you trust God to break your strongholds?

____

____

____

____

____

____

____

____

Verse for prayer and reflection

Psalm 26:2 (NKJV)

2Examine me, O LORD, and prove me; Try my mind and my heart.

We live in a world where Money is Power, but God's Word in 1 Timothy 6:10-11 (NKJV) says:

10For the love of money is a root of all kinds of evil, for which some have strayed from the faith in their greediness, and pierced themselves through with many sorrows.

11But you, O man of God, flee these things and pursue righteousness, godliness, faith, love, patience, gentleness.

Chapter synthesis

In this chapter we discovered that our financial problems are not unique to us alone. God knew we would have financial problems. That is why He helps us to identify our problems. He also gives us hope through His Word. When we are honest with ourselves and with God about our financial problems, we can cast our burdens unto Him. He will give us hope, guidance and direction through His Word on how to make adjustments and changes in our situation.

Suggested Reading

Proverbs: There are 31 chapters of Proverbs packed with enough wisdom for an entire lifetime. Try to read through them once a month. I guarantee you will find something new every time you do.

Hard questions to ask ourselves

1. Am I in financial bondage?
2. What is the cause?
3. Can I trust the Lord to set me free?
4. Have I given control of my finances to God?
5. Am I ready to change my ways?

Flee the things of this world—pursue God!

Prayer of deliverance

Father, we come to You in the name of Your Son, Jesus Christ. We stand on Your Word and ask that the financial bondage and the curse of poverty be broken and lifted from our spirits. We ask that the greed, strife, and dependency on money be raised up and bound from our hearts.

We bind Satan and the spirits of insecurity, fear, doubt, and all other spirits of darkness in the name of Jesus, and with His blood.

We now ask that our hearts be cleansed and revived with financial freedom, wisdom, knowledge, and trust in our Lord Jesus.

We ask that the dependency on Jesus and trust in Him for all our financial needs be placed in our hearts and be covered and protected with the blood of Jesus, here and now and until the end of time.

We ask that You bless each of us with prosperity so abundantly that we know that this has only come about because of walking according to Your promises.

We ask that You give us the desire to return those finances which we do not need, back into the ministries of Your Church, which is the body of Christ. We ask that these financial seeds be multiplied and returned one hundredfold, and continue to flow as promised in Your Word so that Your body knows no lack. The desired result is a continuous process of giving and receiving.

We thank You that You supply all our needs. We stand on Your Word: "God is able to make all grace (every favor and earthly blessing) come to you in abundance, so that you may always and under all circumstances and whatever you need be self-sufficient—possessing enough to require no aid or support and furnished in abundance for every good work and charitable donation," as stated in Second Corinthians 9:8 (Amp.). Amen, Amen and Amen.

Notes and reflections...

Chapter 4: Financial Freedom

In This Chapter

- God vs. mammon ($)
- Choosing freedom
- Financial freedom
- Turning it over to God
- Focusing on and trusting Him
- The process of transformation

God's definition of financial freedom is to be spiritually free from the world's system. As long as our focus is on the things of the world we cannot focus on Him. It is God's desire for us to be free from the things of the world, money or possessions, so we can give our full attention to Him (His Word).

In order to seek and to find God's freedom and His kingdom, we need to make a commitment to know His Word, which is His Will. He wants us to be free from the world's system, to become bondservants to Him. What we need to realize here is that we are already free in the Spirit, but we choose by our own free will to be or not to be enslaved by the world system. Since Jesus made us free, we are free.

We are the righteousness of God in Christ, so how can we not be free? We are slaves if we choose to believe Satan, and remain in slavery to things of the flesh. So we are free indeed, but we must act on God's Word, and therefore act as free men. Why do we have to act on God's Word? Because when we were set free from the things of the world we became servants to God, and must therefore follow His commandments and instruction.

To reap the benefits of being one of God's chosen children, we can no longer neglect any part of His Word or His statutes and commandments. As long as we neglect them we are tossed right into the midst of the spiritual battle. Consequently, we will be miserable in that position. We must accept the fact that the battle was over a long time ago, and victory is ours through Christ Jesus. His Word does not say the battle *will be over*, it says *it is over*. It is time that we realize who we are in Christ—that we are joint heirs to the kingdom. God wants us to accept the fact that we are free. Freedom is ours, not *will be* (which includes financial freedom), but we must act on His promises and trust him.

To reap the benefits of being one of God's chosen, we can no longer neglect any part of His Word, statutes or commandments.

If we are ready and sincere about stepping into financial freedom, we have to make a commitment to believe God's Word and to walk in this freedom no matter what happens. Remember, with God all things are possible. Therefore, when we make the commitment to Him that from this day forward we will walk in financial freedom according to all that is written in His Word, all there is left for us to do is trust Him and He will do the rest. His Word says He will, not *someday*, but right *now* because He does not change His Word. His Word is true and therefore He will do it. The key for us is to trust Him. Let us turn things over to Jesus. Let us confess in our hearts that we are free. Let us ask God to forgive us for having acted in unbelief by operating in the flesh as far as our finances are concerned. We are free and do not need to put up with Satan's schemes. We need to let go and put the past behind us. It is part of our human, sinful nature, to focus on the problem rather than on God. When we realize that we cannot solve the problem without God's help, we recognize that He alone is our source, and we must look to Him for direction. If we instead choose to focus on the problem, the problem in turn will consume us and we will be unable to focus on Him.

God's Word promises to deliver us out of all our afflictions—not some, but all. The Word of God is so powerful that we should humble ourselves before Him and ask Him to forgive us for not trusting Him.

God's promises reveal that He has provided for us here and now with not only what we need, and what we want, but also with health, prosperity, and whatever we desire. We all can enjoy the full benefits of these promises, provided we surrender our lives to God. We must accept the new birth and live in this present world according to the Gospel of Christ.

We need to make a commitment to get right with God by studying His Word. If we can live according to His Word, His blessing will be greater than we can receive. The questions of whether His Word is true will be settled once and for all. God's Word is truth. It is a contract wherein He states His promises, and also what He requires of us. All we need to do is our part. We can rest assured that if we do our part, God will do His. He is sovereign and He does not lie.

It is God's will for us to prosper. His Word abundantly promises that we can have everything that is good. God wants us to have whatever we ask for that is within the scope of His will.

This is an absolute promise, which must be true since we know that the Word of God is truth. The only condition is that we believe and have no doubts. Satan comes in and says to us that this is not possible; we must *see* proof before we believe it. That is not what God's Word says.

We should practice asking, in every situation of our lives, "What does God's Word say about this?" We must believe that His Word is the only truth there is. When Satan tries to get us to reason, we need to resist him with the Word. We need to learn to distinguish good from evil and resist the devil. God's Word is true, so His promises must be true.

We need to make a commitment unto God that we will believe His promises and all of His Word. All that is required of us is to believe His Word and act on it and resist Satan—who constantly tries to divert our attention away from God to the evil things of the world.

Many of God's promises contain His unconditional guarantee pronounced by His Words "I will." Other promises are that He will never forsake us, He will guide us, and He will keep our path straight. Just remember that God cannot break His Word.

It is God's will for us to prosper. He promises to bless us with prosperity, but there are some basic requirements. *We must abide by His Word.* We must live according to His Words, which means that it is up to us to take action and learn as much as we can about Him from His Word. How else can we know what His Word says and what His will is unless we commit to the renewing of our mind? Everything we know about His kingdom has been revealed to us by and through His divine Word. Jesus told us that God knows everything that we need, but that we are first to seek His Kingdom and all these things (all good things of life) will be added to us.

God tells us that we need to trust Him no matter what. We are not to depend on our own understanding. When we rely on our own understanding, we allow Satan to cause us to reason, which leads to unbelief. It is very difficult to trust anyone, especially when we do not understand. However, this is the key. We are not to trust our own understanding but trust in Him. This means that we have to deny our self, and yield to God. This is the hardest part of living in the flesh and according to God's Word.

We must build up our trust in Him because without understanding or applied reasoning, we are vulnerable. To build up trust in Him above our own understanding, we must know His Word in our hearts and in our minds. It is then, when we live by His Word, that His Word gives us spiritual confidence. His will is above all, even if we do not intellectually understand. Again, it takes a commitment to know His Word and a constant denial of our selfish nature. Jesus is the light of the world. Jesus is the way. We cannot let ourselves be consumed by the problems of the world. We must remember that Jesus is the answer for the world. We have to trust Him and keep our focus on Him, and on Him only.

In this chapter we will explore the scriptures that assure us of our freedom, and that includes financial freedom. We will also discuss a three-step process to transform our situation into the financial freedom which He promises in His Word.

GOD vs. mammon ($)

God vs. mammon is the dilemma every Christian is faced with today.

Matthew 6:24 (NKJV)

24"No one can serve two masters; for either he will hate the one and love the other, or else he will be loyal to the one and despise the other. You cannot serve God and mammon."

Money is dangerous because it deceives us into thinking that wealth is the easiest way to get everything we want. The love of money is sinful because we trust money, rather than God, to solve our problems. Those who pursue its empty promises will one day discover that they have nothing because they are spiritually bankrupt.—**From the Handbook of Bible Application**

We must choose freedom

Deuteronomy 30: 15 (NASB)

15See, I have set before you today life and prosperity, and death and adversity...

Deuteronomy 30:19-20 (NKJV)

19I call heaven and earth as witnesses today against you, that I have set before you life and death, blessing and cursing; therefore choose life, that both you and your descendants may live; 20that you may love the LORD your God, that you may obey His voice, and that you may cling to Him, for He is your life and the length of your days; and that you may dwell in the land which the LORD swore to your fathers, to Abraham, Isaac, and Jacob, to give them.

What would *financial freedom* look like in your life? What changes would take place?

____

____

____

____

____

____

____

We are called to freedom

Galatians 5:13 (NASB)

13 For you were called to freedom, brethren; only do not turn your freedom into an opportunity for the flesh, but through love serve one another.

Jesus is the only answer

John 14:27 (NKJV)

27 Peace I leave with you, My peace I give to you; not as the world gives do I give to you. Let not your heart be troubled, neither let it be afraid.

John 16:33 (NKJV)

33 These things I have spoken to you, that in Me you may have peace. In the world you will have tribulation; but be of good cheer, I have overcome the world.

2 Corinthians 9:8 (NASB)

8 And God is able to make all grace abound to you, so that always having all sufficiency in everything, you may have an abundance for every good deed...

How does Jesus have the answer to your problems?

____

____

____

____

____

____

____

____

Galatians 5:16-17 (NASB)

[16]But I say, walk by the Spirit, and you will not carry out the desire of the flesh. [17]For the flesh sets its desire against the Spirit, and the Spirit against the flesh; for these are in opposition to one another, so that you may not do the things that you please.

Galatians 6:7-8 (NKJV)

[7]Do not be deceived, God is not mocked; for whatever a man sows, that he will also reap. [8]For he who sows to his flesh will of the flesh reap corruption, but he who sows to the Spirit will of the Spirit reap everlasting life.

"'I say to you, do not worry about your life …' Our Lord says to be careful only about one thing—our relationship to Him. But our common sense shouts loudly and says, 'That is absurd!

I *must* consider how I am going to live, and I *must* consider what I am going to eat and drink.' Jesus says you must not. Beware of allowing yourself to think that He says this while not understanding your circumstances."

—Oswald Chambers, *My Utmost for His Highest*

Financial Freedom

1 John 2:15 (NKJV)

[15]Do not love the world or the things in the world. If anyone loves the world, the love of the Father is not in him.

Matthew 6:31-34 (NASB)

[31]"Do not worry then, saying, 'What will we eat?' or 'What will we drink?' or 'What will we wear for clothing?' [32]For the Gentiles eagerly seek all these things; for your heavenly Father knows that you need all these things. [33]But seek first His kingdom and His righteousness, and all these things will be added to you.
[34]So do not worry about tomorrow; for tomorrow will care for itself. Each day has enough trouble of its own."

Seek first the Kingdom of God

Galatians 5:1 (NASB)

[1]It was for freedom that Christ set us free; therefore keep standing firm and do not be subject again to a yoke of slavery.

John 8:36 (NKJV)

[36]Therefore if the Son makes you free, you shall be free indeed.

Psalm 37:5 (NKJV)

[5]Commit your way to the LORD, Trust also in Him, And He shall bring it to pass.

Romans 8:21 (NKJV)

[21]because the creation itself also will be delivered from the bondage of corruption into the glorious liberty of the children of God.

Romans 6:18, 22 (NKJV)

18*And having been set free from sin, you became slaves of righteousness....*22*But now having been set free from sin, and having become slaves of God, you have your fruit to holiness, and the end, everlasting life.*

Take the time to thank the Lord for setting you free from financial bondage.

Slave of Righteousness

Isaiah 58:6-11 (NKJV)

[6]"Is this not the fast that I have chosen: To loose the bonds of wickedness, To undo the heavy burdens, To let the oppressed go free, And that you break every yoke? [7]Is it not to share your bread with the hungry, And that you bring to your house the poor who are cast out; When you see the naked, that you cover him, And not hide yourself from your own flesh? [8]Then your light shall break forth like the morning, your healing shall spring forth speedily, And your righteousness shall go before you; The glory of the LORD shall be your rear guard. [9]Then you shall call, and the LORD will answer; You shall cry, and He will say, 'Here I am.' If you take away the yoke from your midst, The pointing of the finger, and speaking wickedness, [10]If you extend your soul to the hungry And satisfy the afflicted soul, Then your light shall dawn in the darkness, And your darkness shall be as the noonday. [11]The LORD will guide you continually and satisfy your soul in drought, And strengthen your bones; You shall be like a watered garden, And like a spring of water, whose waters do not fail."

If you do these five things (Isaiah 58: 9, 10 NASB):

1. If you remove the yoke from your midst (through prayer and fasting—Isaiah 58:6 says that fasting undoes the bonds of the yoke and lets the oppressed go free and breaks the bonds of *every yoke*)

2. If you stop pointing the finger *(at the problem)*

3. If you stop speaking the problem

4. If you give yourself to the hungry

5. If you satisfy the desire of the afflicted

Then you will experience freedom in twelve different ways (Isaiah 58: 8-11):

1. Then your light will rise in darkness and your gloom will become like midday

2. Then your light will break out like the dawn

3. Then your recovery will speedily spring forth

4. Then your righteousness will go before you
5. Then the glory of the Lord will be your rear guard
6. Then when you call, the Lord will answer
7. Then when you cry, He will say, "Here I am"
8. Then the Lord will continually guide you
9. Then He will satisfy your desires in scorched places
10. Then He will give strength to your bones
11. Then you will be like a watered garden
12. Then you will be like a spring of water, whose waters do not fail

Three steps to financial freedom

There are three very important steps to follow to help you on your way to financial freedom.

Step 1. Turn things over to God

Psalm 86:5 (NKJV)

5For You, Lord, are good, and ready to forgive, and abundant in mercy to all those who call upon You.

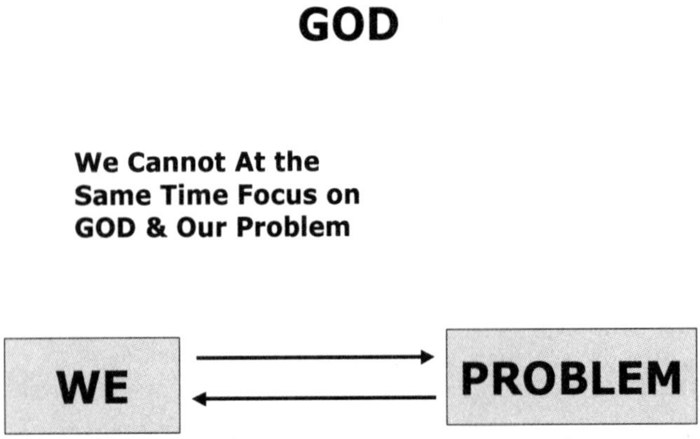

IF WE FOCUS ON OUR FINANCIAL PROBLEMS, THEY WILL IN TURN CONSUME US

Take the time to thank the Lord for setting you free from financial bondage.

Matthew 14:30 (NLT)

[30]But when he (Peter) looked around at the high waves, he was terrified and began to sink. "Save me, Lord!" he shouted.

John 5:2-9 (NLT)

*[2]Inside the city, near the Sheep Gate, was the pool of Bethesda,
with five covered porches. [3]Crowds of sick people—blind, lame,
or paralyzed—lay on the porches. [5]One of the men lying there
had been sick for thirty-eight years. [6]When Jesus saw him and
knew how long he had been ill, he asked him, "Would you like
to get well?"*

[7]"I can't, sir," the sick man said, "for I have no one to help me into the pool when the water is stirred up."

[8]Jesus told him, "Stand up, pick up your sleeping mat, and walk!"

[9]Instantly, the man was healed! He rolled up the mat and began walking! But this miracle happened on the Sabbath day.

Matthew 11:29-30 NLT

*[29]Take my yoke upon you. Let me teach you, because I am humble
and gentle, and you will find rest for your souls. [30]For my yoke
fits perfectly, and the burden I give you is light.*

Commentary on John 5:2-9

Notice there was a crowd of sick people but only one was willing to focus his attention on Jesus. The rest focused on the water. Notice also, that the miraculous healing of this man did *not* stop the multitude from focusing on the pool. They were so busy and into themselves that they did not even notice Jesus.

Compare this to the multitudes who sit around waiting to win the lottery or waiting for someone else to come along to fix their financial problems.

Do you wish to get well? Are you ready to listen to Jesus and roll up your mat and walk?

Proverbs 1:32 (NASB) The complacency of fools will destroy them.

Proverbs 23:7(a) (NASB) For as he thinks within himself, so he is. He says to you, "Eat and drink!" But his heart is not with you.

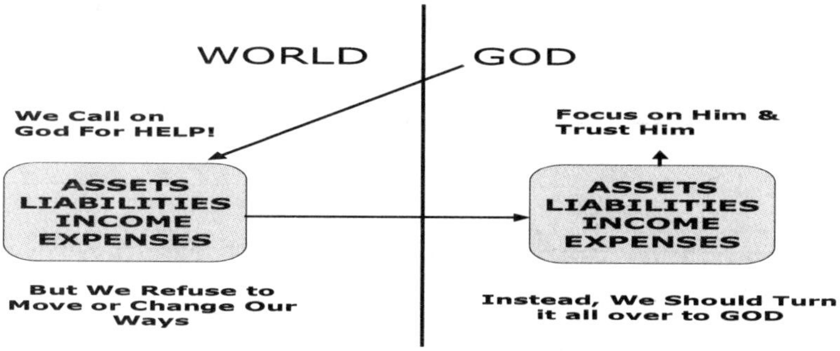

Here we attempt to move God over to our point of view about finances, to get God to do what we want done and to use Him as a means to our end.	We ought to seek to discover God's point of view about finances and learn how, when, and where He wants us to move, live, and manage our finances...and obey.

Step 2. Let go and let God

1 Corinthians 12:2 (NKJV)

2 You know that you were Gentiles, carried away to these dumb idols, however you were led.

Isaiah 43:18 (NKJV)

18 Do not remember the former things, Nor consider the things of old.

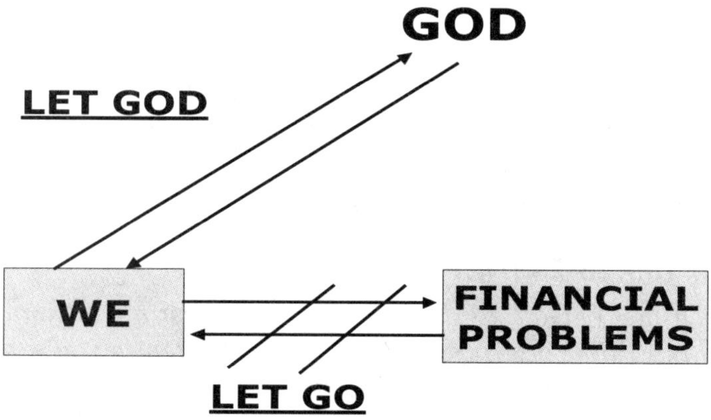

What are some of the "dumb idols" in your life?

____

____

____

____

____

____

____

____

Psalm 46:10-11 (NKJV)

10 Be still, and know that I am God; I will be exalted among the nations, I will be exalted in the earth!
11 The LORD of hosts is with us; The God of Jacob is our refuge. ***Selah***

Selah means pause, to meditate

Psalm 100:3 (NKJV)

3 Know that the LORD, He is God; It is He who has made us, and not we ourselves; We are His people and the sheep of His pasture.

Psalm 37:7, 9 (NLT)

7 Be still in the presence of the LORD, and wait patiently for him to act. Don't worry about evil people who prosper or fret about their wicked schemes...
9 For the wicked will be destroyed, but those who trust in the LORD will possess the land.

Psalm 139:23-24 (NLT)

23 Search me, O God, and know my heart; test me and know my thoughts.
24 Point out anything in me that offends you, and lead me along the path of everlasting life.

Read these verses and write down the verbs that we can actively use to trust God, e.g., be still, exalt Him, Know Him as God. Then meditate on each one.

____

____

____

____

____

____

____

____

Step 3. Focus on Him and trust Him

Psalm 32:8 (NASB)

8 I will instruct you and teach you in the way which you should go; I will counsel you with My eye upon you.

Proverbs 3:5 (NKJV)

5 Trust in the LORD with all your heart, And lean not on your own understanding;

Proverbs 16:9 (NKJV)

9 A man's heart plans his way, But the LORD directs his steps.

Joshua 1:5 (NKJV)

5 No man shall be able to stand before you all the days of your life; as I was with Moses, so I will be with you. I will not leave you nor forsake you.

Trust = Unwavering Faith

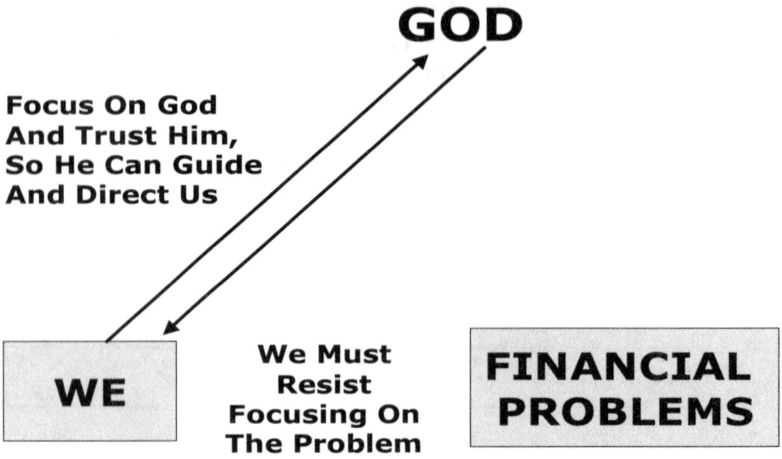

What can you do to practice trusting God?

____

____

____

____

____

____

____

____

Trust in the Lord

Proverbs 28:13 (NASB)

[13]He who conceals his transgressions will not prosper, but he who confesses and forsakes them will find compassion.

Proverbs 28:25 (NKJV)

[25]He who is of a proud heart stirs up strife, But he who trusts in the LORD will be prospered.

Financial freedom is freedom from debt, from poverty, from never having enough and moving into living an abundant life in prosperity.

Achieving Financial Freedom is in most cases a process of transformation.

- The basic level where most people with financial problems are stuck is: Never having enough
- The next level can be summed up as having just enough.
- The next higher level can be summed up as having more than enough.

But the ultimate level of financial freedom is:

- Having an abundance to give and share.

The process of transformation

Build your faith in God—through the Word

Hebrews 4:12 (NKJV)

12For the Word of God is living and powerful, and sharper than any two-edged sword, piercing even to the division of soul and spirit, and of joints and marrow, and is a discerner of the thoughts and intents of the heart.

Romans 10:17 (NKJV)

17So then faith comes by hearing, and hearing by the word of God.

Romans 10:10 (NLT)

10For it is by believing in your heart that you are made right with God, and it is by confessing with your mouth that you are saved.

Proverbs 28:20(a) (NKJV)

[20]A faithful man will abound with blessings.

Soul = Mind Will Emotions

Walking in the Spirit—is to live in Christ

We are a new creation of the Kingdom of God. We need to learn and know how to walk under the laws that govern His Spiritual Kingdom. By studying the Word of God, we feed our spirit. When we learn the laws, rules, and regulations that govern the spiritual realm, we gain knowledge of how to rule and govern the natural world.

Galatians 5:16-17, 25 (NKJV)

[16]I say then: Walk in the Spirit, and you shall not fulfill the lust of the flesh. [17]For the flesh lusts against the Spirit, and the Spirit against the flesh; and these are contrary to one another, so that you do not do the things that you wish.... [25]If we live in the Spirit, let us also walk in the Spirit.

Romans 8:5-6 (NASB)

[5]For those who are according to the flesh set their minds on the things of the flesh, but those who are according to the Spirit, the things of the Spirit. [6]For the mind set on the flesh is death, but the mind set on the Spirit is life and peace.

Chapter synthesis

2 Corinthians 3:17 (NASB)

17Now the Lord is the Spirit; and where the Spirit of the Lord is, there is liberty.

It is time to tear down strongholds and fill the vacant places with love, joy, peace, prosperity, and blessings. We *can* develop a desire to tithe, a desire to give, a desire for goodness, a desire to lavish others with kindness, and a desire to receive gracefully.

Freedom, including financial freedom, belongs to us who believe. As we saw in this chapter, as long as we do our part, God will always do His part. Financial freedom is liberty and it does belong to us. We are not required to remain in financial bondage. To the contrary, we are already free indeed.

Father God, our needs are met as promised in Your Word so that Your body knows no lack. The desired result is a continuous process of giving and receiving.

We thank You that You supply all our needs. We stand on Your Word: "God is able to make all grace (every favor and earthly blessing) come to you in abundance, so that you may always and under all circumstances and whatever you need be self-sufficient—possessing enough to require no aid or support and furnished in abundance for every good work and charitable donation" as stated in Second Corinthians 9:8 (Amp.). Amen, Amen and Amen.

Notes and reflections...

Chapter 5: Ownership and Stewardship

In This Chapter

- What is stewardship?
- What is wealth?
- What does God expect from us?
- What can we expect from God?

When we think of wealth we immediately think of money or material possessions. We have been conditioned to reason that way. *True wealth is what is in the heart of man.* Love, joy, peace, health, to mention a few, are gifts of God and cannot be measured by money or obtained with money. We all have heard at one time or another that someone was ill and that all the money in the world could not buy his health. Another example is that often the rich are very unhappy and even money cannot buy peace, joy, or happiness. Therefore wealth, as it consists of material things, has only limited value to us.

Who created wealth and who owns it? God created it all, He owns it all. Why then do we get so greedy and selfish about ownership of material possessions? Again, Satan who leads us to believe that we own things has told us lies. We need to recognize that God's Word says that *He* owns everything, and that we are joint heirs to all things through Christ Jesus. We do not need to have our names on things. Personal ownership has no real value. We have never seen anyone take anything with them when they died. Without the need for personal ownership there would be no greed, jealousy, strife or theft. In reality, we do not own anything at all; we are only stewards of that which God entrusts to us.

God is telling us that it is far better to do good and to share. This results in a solid foundation for the future, whereas the riches of this world are only temporary.

God clearly warns us that riches will not count in the day of wrath, and that he who trusts in riches will fall. The dilemma is that we must choose between God and mammon. If we continue to choose to place our trust in possessions (riches), He assures us that we will fall. It is imperative that we recognize this while there is time, and put our trust in God.

We need to understand that the Lord warns us of what will happen if we worship other gods and idols such as money. We need to repent, ask for His forgiveness and turn back to serving Him. In summation, God wants us to turn back to Him. If we lack the wisdom to accomplish what he wants, Jesus told us to ask and He will give it to us.

Put your focus on Him

The Father has promised to give us wealth, and gladly the kingdom too. That is true as long as we put our focus on Him and not on the things of this world. When our eyes are fixed on the riches of the world, it is very difficult, if not impossible, to give up those riches and focus on Him.

Remember, the riches of this world are not forever. Satan uses this situation to generate a fear of losing it all. The pure fact remains that Satan has deceived us with regard to our finances. We have accepted poverty and riches without examining who our source is. We need to understand that the only true source to meet our needs abundantly is God. Persons prompted by

Satan can use money too, and he will do anything to keep us from the righteousness of God. Let us examine our hearts, bind Satan and refocus on Jesus.

In this chapter we will review the scriptures that teach us about ownership and stewardship. As previously established, God is the creator and owner of all things. We need to understand that material things, as well as the money which we possess, in reality belong to God. It is by His grace that we have what we have. Stewardship then must be defined as managing those things that have been entrusted to us. This gives a perspective of stewardship rather than ownership. We are required to manage the things and money that belong to God. *We are His trustees, and along with this comes responsibility, accountability, and faithfulness. As stewards we must also be trustworthy.*

The choices are very clear. In the past we have chosen the world's way, which was obviously wrong. We must now choose God's way. Once we know and understand a principle of God, we must follow His way, for the consequences are too grave to do otherwise.

We also must be willing to accept God's direction, which is stated throughout the Word. This, again, puts the responsibility for action on us to get to know the will of God, which comes by reading, meditating on, and following His Word.

Definition of Steward:

One who manages another's property, finances, or other affairs. (Dictionary.com)

What is stewardship?

Stewardship or trusteeship means—managing those things which have been entrusted to us.

This definition gives a perspective of *stewardship*, not *ownership*.

The extent of our authority is as stewards who manage what has been entrusted by God.

We are stewards of that which God entrusted to us!

Psalm 8:4, 6 (NKJV)

4What is man that You are mindful of him, and the son of man that You visit him? You have made him to have dominion over the works of Your hands; You have put all things under his feet.

Psalm 115:16 (NKJV)

16The heaven, even the heavens, are the LORD's; But the earth He has given to the children of men.

Do you view yourself as an owner or as a steward? Why?

___

___

___

___

___

___

___

___

___

___

___

As stewards we must be accountable

Luke 16:1-2 (NKJV)

[1]He also said to His disciples: "There was a certain rich man who had a steward, and an accusation was brought to him that this man was wasting his goods. [2]So he called him and said to him, 'What is this I hear about you? Give an account of your stewardship, for you can no longer be steward.'

Matthew 25:14-15, 19-29 (NKJV)

[14]"For the kingdom of heaven is like a man traveling to a far country, who called his own servants and delivered his goods to them. [15]And to one he gave five talents, to another two, and to another one, ***to each according to his own ability****; and immediately he went on a journey.*

[19]After a long time the lord of those servants came and settled accounts with them.

[20]So he who had received five talents came and brought five other talents, saying, 'Lord, you delivered to me five talents; look, I have gained five more talents besides them.' [21]His lord said to him, 'Well done, good and faithful servant; you were faithful over a few things, I will make you ruler over many things. Enter into the joy of your lord.' [22]He also who had received two talents came and said, 'Lord, you delivered to me two talents; look, I have gained two more talents besides them.' [23]His lord said to him, 'Well done, good and faithful servant; you have been faithful over a few things, I will make you ruler over many things. Enter into the joy of your lord.'"

[24]"Then he who had received the one talent came and said, 'Lord, I knew you to be a hard man, reaping where you have not sown, and gathering where you have not scattered seed. [25]And I was afraid, and went and hid your talent in the ground. Look, there you have what is yours.' [26]But his lord answered and said to him, 'You wicked and lazy servant, you knew that I reap where I have not sown, and gather where I have not scattered seed. [27]So you ought to have deposited my money with the bankers, and at my coming I would have received back my own with interest. [28]So take the talent from him, and give it to him who has ten talents.'

29*For to everyone who has, more will be given, and he will have abundance; but from him who does not have, even what he has will be taken away."*

Let's say a talent equals $1,000. How would you manage five, two, or one talent(s), and why?

If you were asked to give an accounting of your stewardship, what would you say?

As stewards we must be faithful

Luke 8:18 (NKJV)

*[18]Therefore take heed how you hear. For whoever has, to him
more will be given; and whoever does not have, even what he
seems to have will be taken from him.*

Luke 16:10-15 (NASB)

*[10]"He who is faithful in a very little thing is faithful also in
much; and he who is unrighteous in a very little thing is
unrighteous also in much. [11]"Therefore if you have not been
faithful in the use of unrighteous wealth, who will entrust the
true riches to you? [12]And if you have not been faithful in the use
of that which is another's, who will give you that which is your
own? [13]No servant can serve two masters; for either he will hate
the one and love the other, or else he will be devoted to one and
despise the other. You cannot serve God and wealth." [14]Now the
Pharisees, who were lovers of money, were listening to all these
things and were scoffing at Him. [15]And He said to them, "You
are those who justify yourselves in the sight of men, but God
knows your hearts; for that which is highly esteemed among
men is detestable in the sight of God."*

Luke 12:42-44 (NASB)

*[42]And the Lord said, "Who then is the faithful and sensible
steward, whom his master will put in charge of his servants, to
give them their rations at the proper time? [43]Blessed is that slave
whom his master finds so doing when he comes. [44]Truly I say to
you that he will put him in charge of all his possessions."*

2 Timothy 2:15 (NASB)

*[15]Be diligent to present yourself approved to God as a workman
who does not need to be ashamed, accurately handling the word
of truth.*

Using the above verses to guide you, what can you do to become a more faithful steward?

____

____

____

____

____

____

____

____

> Faith comes by hearing the Word of God.
> Faithful = Full of Faith

As stewards we must be trustworthy

1 Corinthians 4:2 (NASB)

2In this case, moreover, it is required of stewards that one be found trustworthy.

As stewards, we must also be responsible

James 4:17 (NLT)

17Remember, it is sin to know what you ought to do and then not do it.

We must be willing to accept God's direction, stated throughout His Word.

Honesty Time

- How well do you manage your finances?
- Do you have a plan?
- Do you have a budget?
- How often do you look at it?
- Do you keep track of how much you spend?
- Do you know how much you spent in the last three days?

What are your thoughts on stewardship?

____

____

____

____

____

____

____

____

When your stewardship is lacking, it can make your spending cycle more like a treadmill

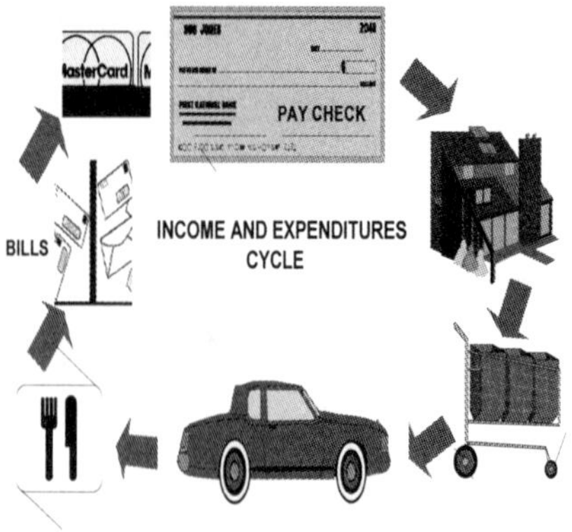

What is wealth?

Where did it come from?

The world's definition of wealth is money or material possessions—these are all *temporary*.

God's definition of wealth is what is in the heart of man—this wealth is *permanent*.

Love, joy and peace cannot be bought with money.

Do you remember...

Proverbs 23:4-5 (NASB)

[4]Do not weary yourself to gain wealth, Cease from your consideration of it. [5]When you set your eyes on it, it is gone. For wealth certainly makes itself wings Like an eagle that flies toward the heavens.

Psalm 49:10 (NASB)

[10]For he sees that even wise men die; the stupid and the senseless alike perish and leave their wealth to others.

You can't take it with you!

Who created things?

Psalm 146:6 (NKJV)

[6]Who made heaven and earth, The sea, and all that is in them; Who keeps truth forever;

Isaiah 44:24 (NKJV)

[24]Thus says the LORD, your Redeemer, And He who formed you from the womb: "I am the LORD, who makes all things, Who stretches out the heavens all alone, Who spreads abroad the earth by Myself..."

Memorize this verse:

Revelation 4:11 (NKJV)

[11]"You are worthy, O Lord, To receive glory and honor and power; For You created all things, And by Your will they exist and were created."

If you had $1,000,000, what would you do differently?

Who owns things?

1 Chronicles 29:11-12 (NKJV)

*11 Yours, O LORD, is the greatness, The power and the glory ,The
victory and the majesty; For all that is in heaven and in earth
is Yours; Yours is the kingdom, O LORD, And You are exalted as
head over all.*

*12 Both riches and honor come from You, And You reign over all.
In Your hand is power and might; In Your hand it is to make
great And to give strength to all.*

Psalm 50:10-12 (NKJV)

*10 For every beast of the forest is Mine, And the cattle on a
thousand hills. 11 I know all the birds of the mountains, And the
wild beasts of the field are Mine. 12 If I were hungry, I would not
tell you; For the world is Mine, and all its fullness.*

What does God say about money?

1 Timothy 6:17-19 (NASB)

*17 Instruct those who are rich in this present world not to be
conceited or to fix their hope on the uncertainty of riches, but on
God, who richly supplies us with all things to enjoy. 18 Instruct*

them to do good, to be rich in good works, to be generous and ready to share, [19]*storing up for themselves the treasure of a good foundation for the future, so that they may take hold of that which is life indeed.*

Proverbs 11:4 (NKJV)

[4]*Riches do not profit in the day of wrath, But righteousness delivers from death.*

Proverbs 11:28 (NASB)

[28]*He who trusts in his riches will fall, but the righteous will flourish like the green leaf.*

Be rich in good works

What does God expect from *us*?

Proverbs 3:4-6 (NKJV)

[4]*And so find favor and high esteem In the sight of God and*
man.[5]*Trust in the LORD with all your heart, And lean not on*
your own understanding; [6]*In all your ways acknowledge Him,*
And He shall direct your paths.

Deuteronomy 8:18-19 (NKJV)

[18]*And you shall remember the LORD your God, for it is He who*
gives you power to get wealth, that He may establish His covenant
which He swore to your fathers, as it is this day. [19]*Then it shall*
be, if you by any means forget the LORD your God, and follow
other gods, and serve them and worship them, I testify against
you this day that you shall surely perish.

Trust & Obey

What can *we* expect from God?

Proverbs 8:17-21 (NASB)

Are God's promises true?

17 I love those who love me; And those who diligently seek me will find me.

18 Riches and honor are with me, Enduring wealth and righteousness.

19 My fruit is better than gold, even pure gold, And my yield better than choicest silver.

20 I walk in the way of righteousness, In the midst of the paths of justice,

21 To endow those who love me with wealth, That I may fill their treasuries.

Luke 12:29-32 (NASB)

29 And do not seek what you will eat and what you will drink,
and do not keep worrying. 30 For all these things the nations of
the world eagerly seek; but your Father knows that you need
these things. 31 But seek His kingdom, and these things will be
added to you. 32 Do not be afraid, little flock, for your Father has
chosen gladly to give you the kingdom.

Why should you trust God to supply all of your needs?

____

____

____

____

____

____

____

____

The real dangers of money

1 Timothy 6:10-11 (NKJV)

[10]For the love of money is a root of all kinds of evil, for which some have strayed from the faith in their greediness, and pierced themselves through with many sorrows. [11]But you, O man of God, flee these things and pursue righteousness, godliness, faith, love, patience, gentleness.

Matthew 19:23-24 (NKJV)

[23]Then Jesus said to His disciples, "Assuredly, I say to you that it is hard for a rich man to enter the kingdom of heaven. [24]And again I say to you, it is easier for a camel to go through the eye of a needle than for a rich man to enter the kingdom of God."

Personal inventory time...

Take the time to consider all of the blessings that you have in your life. What is the happiest moment you can remember from your life? What were the attributes of that moment that made you feel content? Who was there? How much money did you spend?

Chapter synthesis

In this chapter, we discovered what God's Word says about ownership and stewardship. We examined the facts about who really owns things. We also reviewed scriptures that give us direction about the responsibilities of stewardship. Stewards must be accountable, trustworthy, responsible, and willing to accept God's direction.

Notes and reflections...

Chapter 6: Rearrange Your Priorities for Financial Success

In This Chapter

- Life Priorities and Financial Priorities
- Relationship with God
- Relationship with spouse
- Relationship with children
- Work/Vocation
- Finances
- Elements of a financial plan

When we think of a long-range financial plan for our household or family, we usually think of it in terms of our future financial needs. However, finances are only part of a family plan. We have been taught to think of almost anything in terms of finances. We must learn to put God first.

The term "long-range" can become confusing to many, when in fact they are struggling to make ends meet today. We have been brainwashed by television to expect instant solutions to everything. During a half-hour program a story begins, a plot develops, and the story concludes. Often we find that things are moving so fast that we do not have time to plan, or it seems useless to plan.

One of the most important steps in long-range planning for a family is that *all members of the family are participating* in the planning. At times plans are developed and then forced upon members of the family. Obviously this can cause confusion, resentment, and defiance. The best approach is to include all members affected from the beginning so that the plan can be established. Remember that God cares about all of us, and it is God's will for us to prosper, not only financially, but as individuals as well.

It is difficult to sit down with the whole family and plan. Sometimes we begin to reason why past planning efforts have failed and why current efforts are just as futile. Then we rationalize that these efforts are incapable of producing useful results. Satan does not want us to plan because God does. God's Word tells us that we should plan. It also says to commit our plans to Him and He will establish them for us. If we then become stable in our ways because of planning, Satan loses ground. Let us not be deceived by our current problems, thinking that we must first take care of them before we can effectively plan. That is not true. We need to make a commitment to start planning today. The current problems will be dealt with within the framework of this plan.

Another difficult problem area in developing a family plan is the husband's ego and pride. Often men feel threatened by the fact that they have to surrender their position of dominance. Men usually hide from their families their own insecurities and vulnerabilities, and thereby keep the family from operating as an entity or cooperative unit. The long-range plan outlined below deals with these deceptions by Satan. *Setting priorities* that work bring the family together into a strong and powerful unit as God intended it to be. God tells us to be strong and courageous, and that He will be with us. He will never fail or forsake us. God also assures us of His presence in our life. When we ask, God hears us and sets our paths straight.

In this chapter we will discuss what the scriptures tell us about *life priorities* and *financial priorities.* The following elements are listed in order of importance. Each category will be discussed in detail.

- Relationship with God
- Relationship with spouse
- Relationship with children
- Work or vocation
- Finances

All these elements are essential for a successful family plan. They are listed in order of importance for a specific reason. When we evaluate our priorities up to this point in our lives, chances are that they are presently not in the same order.

For example, if we put finances as our priority, which often is the case, then we shortchange ourselves to some degree in all of the four preceding categories. That might work for a while, but in the long run the family unit will suffer and often is destroyed. When I reflect on my life, I remember the time when life seemed hopeless, confused and full of chaotic ups and downs.

One day I was driving to a business meeting in a neighboring town about ten miles away. I felt so restless and worried about my family problems, financial problems, and about my whole life in general. In utter despair, I said to God that if He was there that now I needed Him. At that instant a total peace and calm came over me from head to toe. From that day forward I wanted to get *to know Him.*

I started searching for Him—only to realize that He was always here. I found closeness with God when I read the Bible. Then I rationalized that I had so many things to do that in reality there was little time for me to spend reading His Word. After all, there were demands on my time by my work, my spouse, my children and numerous other events and organizations. When I realized that God had to come first, I made a commitment to start each day by reading His Word, to fellowship with Him. As a result, I had more time for the family, plus time to do all things that needed to be done.

The priorities in a family leading to the maximum love, joy, peace and fulfillment must follow the listed order of importance. Without a personal relationship with God nothing else can work right because Satan will destroy it. When we keep our focus on God, and work on improving our personal relationship with Him, in time all five categories will fall into place, one by one.

Relationship with God

As we discussed in an earlier chapter, we need to learn the will of God. We cannot do what God wants us to do unless we learn His Word. To step into freedom is to learn *and* act on God's Word.

Each day as we start out we should humble ourselves before the Lord by praying something like this: Lord, I humble myself before You. I fully surrender to You. I lay my life before You. Please guide and direct me this day according to Your will, not mine, in all things that I do and say.

The Lord knows every thought and intention of our hearts and He answers prayer. Prayer is God's appointed way of obtaining things. The great deficiency in our family relationships, our lives, our work, or whatever, is our lack of prayer.

Reading daily in God's Word is a blessing. Only God can give inner peace, and He promises it if we love His Word.

Relationship with spouse

Men often use it to dominate or dictate to their wives. We must realize that trying to change or dictate to any person is futile. When we focus on the spouse and try to get them to change, all we receive in return is rebellion. It is our human nature by which we defend ourselves when someone is critical about us.

Instead, what we need to do is focus on God, and not on the other person. God told us we should love one another just as we were created in His image. He did not say we should change one another.

The only way we can learn about Christ's love is to learn the Word. We must focus on our personal relationship with God before our relationship with our spouse can come into place. God is the only one who can bring the husband and wife relationship to what He intended it to be, one of great love, joy and peace.

A daily devotional time and prayer together will work wonders. There is nothing more satisfying and fulfilling than husband and wife praying and sharing God's Word together. To do this will be the foundation of good communication between husband and wife.

Relationship with children

Our children are gifts from God. We are the stewards of that which God has entrusted to us. We are responsible to God for how we raise our children.

Whatever we teach our children will be with them for all of their lives. This is true for the good as well as the bad habits. When we watch young children we can see how they imitate their parents. For example, a young boy will watch his father shave and then with total admiration might say: "Dad, I want to be just like you when I grow up." Ephesians Chapter 6 tells us about the family relationship with our children.

Our children need to know and feel that they are loved, just as God loves all of us. If our children see love and harmony in their parents, they will feel secure and loved. On the other hand, when there is strife, anger and hatred between the parents, this will be reflected in the children and their attitudes. It is important for us to realize what impact our relationship with God and with our spouse has on our children. We need to *spend some quality time* with each of them as often as we can, as well as all together as a family.

Work or vocation

A vocation is an occupation regularly followed to make a living. We all know that we are servants of God. A servant is a person employed by another. Therefore, we are employed by God. Jesus told us that a worker is worth his hire. God, in fact, tells us that we should work. Sometimes there is confusion among some Christians as to whether they should work because God's Word says that he will supply all our needs. But God's Word also says that anyone who does not work should not eat.

How can our finances come into order if it is not our priority to work? Satan deceives us by feeding us discouragement and lack of self-esteem to keep us from trying to find work. God told us to work six days, but to rest on the seventh day. Yes, God wants us to work but not at the expense of sacrificing our relationship with Him and with our family.

I have seen people who have put their work above everything. They work six or even seven days a week, and always complain about not having enough time to get everything done. They have become slaves to their work. Their work dictates their lives. They have put their work before God and before their family life. The result is total consumption by work at the expense of a rewarding relationship with God and to the detriment of a strong, healthy and supportive family unit.

If we are unemployed, we need to take courage and come before God and stand on His Word, which says that He wants us to work. We need to tell Him that we are going out today to work for Him. His Word says, seek and you shall find, knock, and it shall be opened to you. His Word is all true because God cannot change it.

God has given to each of us talents. When we begin using these talents, no matter how insignificant they may seem, God will bless the fact that we are using them. As we input and multiply our efforts, which may be slow and discouraging at first, they will be multiplied back to us thirty, sixty and one hundredfold. Hope and faith cannot fail to succeed.

Finances

God wants us to prosper and reap the benefits of our labor. Financial planning and control may be broadly defined as a systematic and formalized approach to accomplishing the planning, coordination and control of responsibilities of the family management. Management of the finances for a family is the coordination of every member's effort to accomplish the goals. This process includes decision-making, the application of selected procedures, and the motivation of every individual in the family to accomplish specific objectives.

Suggested objectives for discussion among all family members are listed below. Pray together with your family about how God wants you to live:

- The house you live in
- The car you drive
- Where you should work
- Whether the wife should work

Establish priorities by discussing among all members these differences:

- Needs
- Wants
- Desires

When you pray, ask God to put your spirits in agreement. Sometimes that takes a while and improves patience, but all things work together for good for those who love the Lord.

The lifestyle a family chooses has to be built around what it is able to afford. We are stewards of that which God has entrusted to us, meaning we have to learn to become content with whatever circumstances are before us. To him who is faithful with a little, more is given.

Suggested goals for a sound financial plan are:

- Living within your means
- Planning to become debt-free
- Establishing a giving program
- Establishing a saving program

Rearranging your financial or spending priorities

When we do rearrange our spending priorities and subject our habits to God's Word, we can begin to operate in financial freedom.

- The first part belongs to God
- The second part belongs to the government
- The third part is to meet our family needs
- The fourth part goes to pay our debts
- The fifth part is to save

God will show us how to deal with the problems and how to solve them.

A few years ago a divorced woman came to see me and asked for financial advice. Her income, in round numbers, was $500 net per month, and her expenses were $700 per month. She had already a first and second mortgage on her house. She thought her only solution was a third mortgage.

She reviewed the priorities mentioned above. She questioned how she could possibly tithe when she was already $200 per month short. Satan had her exactly where he wanted her. When we turn our struggles over to God, He will guide us and lead us through the problems and into the promised freedom. She agreed that no matter how difficult the task to follow these priorities would be, she would stick to it. She began giving a ten-percent tithe to her church. Her taxes were withheld by her employer. She bought only what she needed, such as food, shelter, and clothing. The balance, which was not much, she allocated among her debts. She told her creditors that she would pay as much as she could each month, but that she was going to pay all debts. God started to bless her because she was tithing. In less than two years all credit card debts and the second mortgage were paid off. She shared that all her needs were met each month and that she had no lack of anything. Praise the Lord!

Blessings, just as this one, have been the result in every case where the trust was put in God and His Word.

Correct life priorities

CORRECT LIFE PRIORITIES

1. God
2. Spouse
3. Children
4. Work
5. Finances

**List your own life priorities—
any differences since Chapter 1?**

1.____

2.____

3.____

4.____

5.____

Since we considered priorities in Chapter 1, have you made changes? What results have you seen?

____

____

____

____

____

____

____

____

Setting priorities requires taking a personal inventory

God knows our hearts and motives and attitudes better than we do. Let us search our hearts to evaluate our past and current habits and motives.

Psalm 139:23-24 (NKJV)

[23]Search me, O God, and know my heart; Try me, and know my anxieties;[24]And see if there is any wicked way in me, And lead me in the way everlasting.

Psalm 26:2 (NLT)

[2]Put me on trial, LORD, and cross-examine me. Test my motives and affections.

Proverbs 16:2 (NLT)

[2]People may be pure in their own eyes, but the LORD examines their motives.

2 Corinthians 13:5-6 (NASB)

[5]Test yourselves to see if you are in the faith; examine yourselves! Or do you not recognize this about yourselves, that Jesus Christ

is in you--unless indeed you fail the test? [6]But I trust that you will realize that we ourselves do not fail the test.

When looking at ourselves, it always helps to know that Jesus is with us, for us, and in us. We can do all things through Christ who strengthens us (Phil. 4:13). When we ask Him to help us search our hearts and minds, He will show us in all gentleness where we are.

1. Relationship with God

As we discussed in an earlier chapter, we need to learn the will of God. We cannot do what God wants us to do unless we learn His Word and meditate on it. To step into freedom is to learn to communicate with God and act on His Word. Each day as we start out we should humble ourselves before the Lord praying something like this:

Lord I humble myself before You. I fully surrender myself before You. Please guide me and direct me this day according to Your will, and not my own, in all the things that I do and say. Show me today what is pleasing in Your sight.

Psalm 51:10 & 12 (NASB)

[10]Create in me a clean heart, O God, And renew a steadfast spirit within me. [12]Restore to me the joy of Your salvation And sustain me with a willing spirit.

The Lord answers prayers and He knows every thought and intention of our hearts. Prayer is God's appointed way of relating with Him. The great secret of all lack in our family relationships, our lives, our work, etc., is our lack of prayer. Through the daily reading of God's Word, and honest prayer seeking His face, we have an opportunity to be a part of His blessing.

Psalm 119:165 (NKJV)

[165]Great peace have those who love Your law, and nothing causes them to stumble.

Only God can give inner peace. In fact, He promises it if we love His Word.

Psalm 1:1-3 Paraphrase

Blessed is the man whose delight is in the law of the LORD, and in His law he meditates day and night. He shall be like a tree planted by the rivers of water that brings forth its fruit in season, whose leaves also shall not wither; and whatever he does shall prosper.

What stands in the way of your relationship with God at different times in your life?

____

____

____

____

____

____

____

2. Relationship with spouse

The following verses are very often misunderstood by Christian couples:

Ephesians 5:22-23 (NKJV)

22 Wives, submit to your own husbands, as to the Lord. 23 For the husband is head of the wife, as also Christ is head of the church; and He is the Savior of the body.

Most of us are familiar with these scriptures. Some men use them to dominate or dictate to their wives. However, we must realize that trying to change or dictate to any person is futile. When we focus on our spouse, and try to force them to change, all we receive is resistance or at worst rebellion. It is our human nature by which we defend ourselves when someone is critical about us. Instead what we need to do is focus on God, and not on the other person. God told us we should love one another just as we were created in His image. *He did not say that we should change one another.*

This passage of scripture goes on to say:

Ephesians 5:25 (NKJV)

[25]Husbands, love your wives, just as Christ also loved the church and gave Himself for her.

Christ's love is unconditional. We must therefore love our spouse unconditionally. The only way we can learn about Christ's love is to learn the Word and communicate with Him through prayer throughout each day. We must focus on our personal relationship with God before our relationship with our spouse can come into place.

God is the only one who can bring the husband and wife relationship to what He intended it to be, one of great love, joy, and peace.

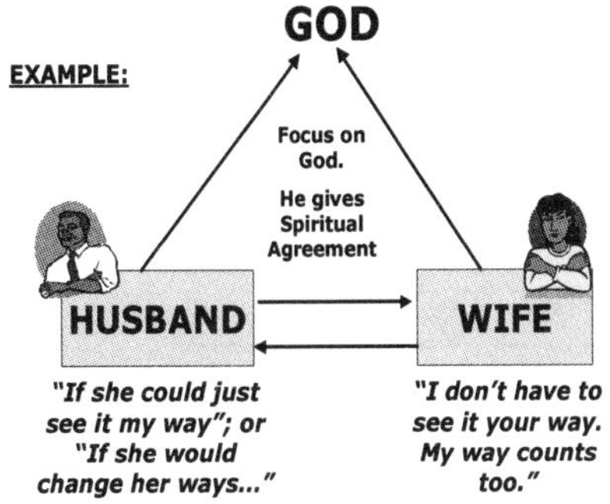

A daily devotional and prayer time together will work wonders in any marriage. There is nothing more satisfying and fulfilling than husband and wife praying and sharing God's word together. When we do this daily, it builds a foundation for communication.

3. Relationship with children

Our children are gifts from God. We are the stewards of that which God has entrusted to us. We are responsible to God for how we raise our children.

Proverbs 22:6 (NKJV)

[6]Train up a child in the way he should go, And when he is old he will not depart from it.

Whatever we teach our children will be with them for all of

their lives. This is true for the good habits as well as the bad ones. When you watch your children, you can see how they imitate their parents. For example, a young boy will watch his father shave and then with total admiration might say: "Dad, I want to be just like you when I grow up."

Our children need to know and feel that they are loved, just as God loves all of us. If our children see love and harmony in their parents they will feel secure and loved. On the other hand, when there is strife, anger, and hatred among the parents this will be reflected in the attitudes of the children.

Colossians 3:12-14 (NKJV—emphasis added)

12 Therefore, as the elect of God, holy and beloved, put on tender mercies, kindness, humility, meekness, longsuffering; 13 bearing with one another, and forgiving one another, if anyone has a complaint against another; even as Christ forgave you, so you also must do. 14 But above all these things put on love, which is the <u>*bond of perfection*</u>*.*

It is important for us to realize what an impact our relationship with God and with our spouse has on their children. We need to make an effort to spend some quality time with each of them individually as often as we can, as well as all together as a family.

> **Further verses to consider on your own:**
>
> Ephesians Chapter 6 tells about the family relationship with our children.

4. Work/Vocation

A vocation is an occupation regularly followed to make a living. We all know that we are servants of God. A servant is a person employed by another. Therefore we are employed by God. Jesus tells us in Luke 10:7 that a worker deserves payment. We are commanded to work. Consider the following verses:

Ruth 2:12 (NLT)

12 May the LORD, the God of Israel, under whose wings you have come to take refuge, reward you fully.

Proverbs 14:23 (NLT)

[23]*Work brings profit, but mere talk leads to poverty!*

Colossians 3:23 (NLT)

[23]*Work hard and cheerfully at whatever you do, as though you were working for the Lord rather than for people.*

Sometimes there is confusion among Christians as to whether or not they should work because God's Word says that He will supply all of our needs (Philippians 4:19). But God's Word also says:

2 Thessalonians 3:10 (NKJV)

[10]*For even when we were with you, we commanded you this: If anyone will not work, neither shall he eat.*

Proverbs 10:4 (NKJV)

[4]*He who has a slack hand becomes poor, But the hand of the diligent makes rich.*

Proverbs 12:11 (NLT)

[11]*Hard work means prosperity; only fools idle away their time.*

Proverbs 18:9 (NASB)

[9]*He also who is slack in his work is brother to him who destroys.*

How can our finances come into order if it is not our priority to work? Satan deceives us by feeding us discouragement and lack of self-esteem to keep us from simply trying.

A balance is needed. Yes, God wants us to work but not at the expense of sacrificing our relationship with Him and with our families.

Exodus 34:21 (NKJV)

[21]*Six days you shall work, but on the seventh day you shall rest; in plowing time and in harvest you shall rest.*

Deuteronomy 8:18 (NLT)

[18]Always remember that it is the LORD your God who gives you power to become rich, and he does it to fulfill the covenant He made with your ancestors.

Psalm 127:2 (NLT)

There is a balance
WORK/REST

[2]It is useless for you to work so hard from early morning until late at night, anxiously working for food to eat; for God gives rest to His loved ones.

If we are ever unemployed, we need to take courage and come before God and stand on His Word, which says that He wants us to work. We need to tell Him every day that we are going out to work for Him, even when our labor is job hunting. His Word says that when we seek we will find, and when we knock on doors, they will be opened for us (paraphrase of Luke 11:9). *His Word is all true and it cannot be changed.*

God has given each of us talents. When we begin to use these talents, no matter how insignificant they may seem, God will bless the fact that we are using them. As we multiply our efforts diligently, it will often be slow and discouraging at first, but they will be multiplied back to us thirty, sixty, and one hundredfold fold (paraphrase of Mark 4:20). *Hope and faith cannot fail to succeed.*

Matthew 21:22 (NLT)

[22]And whatever things you ask in prayer, believing, you will receive.

Proverbs 13:11 (NLT)

[11]Wealth from get-rich-quick schemes quickly disappears; wealth from hard work grows.

Proverbs 22:29 (NLT)

[29]Do you see any truly competent workers? They will serve kings rather than ordinary people.

Further verses to consider on your own:
Psalm 90:17
Psalm 128:2
Proverbs 6:6-8
Proverbs 12:24
Proverbs 21:25-26
Proverbs 28:19

5. Finances

God wants us to prosper and reap the benefits of our labor. Consider the following verse:

Ecclesiastes 5:19 (NLT)

[19]*And it is a good thing to receive wealth from God and the good health to enjoy it. To enjoy your work and accept your lot in life—that is indeed a gift from God.*

Did you see that? When *God* grants wealth, He also gives the gift of health to enjoy it.

A closer look at financial priorities

Mixed-up financial priorities

MIXED-UP FINANCIAL PRIORITIES

- Example:
  - a. Debt
  - b. Investing
  - c. Needs
  - d. Taxes
  - e. God

**List your own financial priorities.
Any changes since Chapter 1?**

1. ______________________________

2. ______________________________

3. ______________________________

4. ______________________________

5. ______________________________

Correct financial priorities

CORRECT FINANCIAL PRIORITIES

- Finances:
  a. God – Tithe
  b. Taxes
  c. Needs
  d. Surplus
     1. Debt
     2. Savings & Investing

**Since we considered financial priorities
in Chapter 1, have you made any changes?
What results have you seen?**

____

____

____

What are the elements of a financial plan?

When we do rearrange our spending priorities, and subject our habits to God's Word, we can begin to operate in financial freedom.

1. The first part belongs to God

Proverbs 3:9-10 (NKJV)

[9]Honor the LORD with your possessions, (see Chapter 4) And with the first fruits of all your increase, (see Chapter 9) [10]So your barns will be filled with plenty, And your vats will overflow with new wine.

2. The second part belongs to the government

Matthew 22:21(b) (NKJV)

...And He said to them, "Render therefore to Caesar the things that are Caesar's, and to God the things that are God's."

Romans 13:7 (NASB)

[7]Render to all what is due them: tax to whom tax is due; custom to whom custom; fear to whom fear; honor to whom honor.

3. The third part is to meet our *needs*

Philippians 4:19 (NASB)

[19]And my God will supply all your needs according to His riches in glory in Christ Jesus.

1 Timothy 5:8 (NKJV)

8 *But if anyone does not provide for his own, and especially for those of his household, he has denied the faith and is worse than an unbeliever.*

4. Surplus (what is left over after tithe, taxes, and needs) goes to:

- **Pay toward your debts (Chapters 7 and 8)**

Proverbs 3:27-28 (Paraphrase)

Do not withhold repayment of your debts, when you have the money to repay it.

- **Save and invest (Chapter 10)**

Chapter synthesis

In this chapter we saw how important it is that we examine our *life priorities* as well as our *financial priorities.* Typically we will find both life and financial priorities out of sync with God's divine order. I challenge each reader to put God first and you will find your priorities lining up with His Word. As a result you will surely be blessed.

What have you learned from this chapter? What steps are you going to take to apply what you've learned?

Notes and reflections…

Chapter 7: Debt—the Problem

In This Chapter

- Borrowing
- Overspending
- Debt is a symptom
- Cosigning
- Auto loans
- Installment loans
- Mortgages
- Refinancing

Now that we know and believe that we have been set free through Christ Jesus, we also know that we are joint heirs with Him and partakers in the blessings of the kingdom. When we accept His blessings, we have no need. When we operate under the blessings, which are His promises, then we will not borrow. There is no need to borrow because He will provide all our needs. He will even give us the desires of our heart, provided we first seek the kingdom of God, meaning we operate in and by His Word.

I am not suggesting her that you do not pay your banker for what you owe. Remember that when assets and liabilities have been turned over to God, we need to learn to be obedient to His direction. The direction may vary, depending on what God's purpose is.

When we operate under the blessings, which are His promises, then we will not borrow.

When we do not believe in the blessings promised in His Word, and then we choose to operate under the curse. Then we do things our way and we will borrow. We come under the curse because of disobedience and disbelief.

To become free then we need to get out of debt. As long as we have debt, we are in bondage and subject to problems that come with it, as we are told in Proverbs. **When we borrow, financial bondage occurs**. This is a spiritual bondage that takes place between the one who lends and the one who borrows. If you do not believe you are in bondage due to debt, get three payments behind-then you will notice that the obligation will not be a blessing to either party.

We must break the spiritual bondage between us and the lender. The spiritual realm precedes the physical manifestation. We must forgive and release. We need to ask God to let His unconditional forgiveness flow from Him through our hearts, and cleanse our hearts, as we forgive and release the lender. Then we ask that His unconditional forgiveness flow from Him through the heart, and cleanse the heart, of the lender involved, and to flow forgiveness and release to us. The spiritual bondage is broken and the physical will manifest itself.

We must make a commitment to get out of debt. The freedom and peace we will feel when that is accomplished is difficult to put into words. God will see us through and teach us how to get along without borrowing. As soon as we make a commitment to get out of debt, Satan will put the pressure on to keep us in debt. This is a spiritual battle that is over. It was won by Jesus Christ. The best way to keep the pressure off is to keep our promise to pay. God knows we made these promises, and when we commit our ways to Him, and trust Him He will see to it that the old obligations get paid.

A commitment to get out of debt will only be meaningful if we also agree not to borrow again. God will see us through if we are sincere. He knows our hearts and our intentions. If we are looking for Him to bail us out and immediately get into borrowing again, it will not work. The borrowing can be avoided if we take into consideration what Jesus said. The same principles apply to co-signing. We should not co-sign no matter what the circumstances, because it is the same as borrowing.

Is Debt a Problem?

Definitions from Easton's Bible Dictionary

Debt The Mosaic law encouraged the practice of lending (Deut. 15:7; Ps. 37:26; Matt. 5:42); but it forbade the exaction of interest except from foreigners. Usury [collecting interest] was strongly condemned (Prov. 28:8; Ezek. 18:8, 13, 17; 22:12; Ps. 15:5). On the Sabbatical year all pecuniary [monetary] obligations were canceled (Deut. 15:1-11). These regulations prevented the accumulation of debt.

Debtor Various regulations as to the relation between debtor and creditor are laid down in the scriptures.

The debtor was to deliver up as a pledge to the creditor what he could most easily dispense with (Deut. 24:10, 11).

A mill, or millstone, or upper garment, when given as a pledge, could not be kept over night (Ex. 22:26, 27).

A debt could not be exacted [demanded] during the Sabbatic year (Deut. 15:1-15). For other laws bearing on this relation see Lev. 25:14, 32, 39; Matt. 18:25, 34.

A surety [co-signor] was liable in the same way as the original debtor (Prov. 11:15; 17:18).

Loan The Mosaic law required that when an Israelite needed to borrow, what he asked was to be freely lent to him, and no interest was to be charged, although interest might be taken of a foreigner (Ex. 22:25; Deut. 23:19, 20; Lev. 25:35-38). At the end of seven years all debts were remitted [forgiven]. Of a foreigner the loan might, however, be exacted. At a later period of the Hebrew commonwealth, when commerce increased, the practice of exacting usury or interest on loans, and of surety-ship in the commercial sense, grew up. Yet the exaction of it from a Hebrew was regarded as discreditable (Ps. 15:5; Prov. 6:1, 4; 11:15; 17:18; 20:16; 27:13; Jer. 15:10).

Limitations are prescribed by the law to the taking of a pledge from the borrower.

The outer garment in which a man slept at night, if taken in pledge, was to be returned before sunset (Ex. 22:26, 27; Deut. 24:12, 13). A widow's garment (Deut. 24:17) and a millstone (Deut. 24:6) could not be taken. A creditor could not enter the house to reclaim a pledge, but must remain outside till the borrower brought it (Deut. 24:10, 11). The Hebrew debtor could not be retained in bondage longer than the seventh year, or at farthest the year of jubilee (Ex. 21:2; Lev. 25:39, 42), but foreign sojourners were to be "bondsmen forever" (Lev. 25:44-54).

Food for thought:

The Hebrew word for "borrow" or "lend" in the Old Testament is also at times translated—"to join with" or "attached to". This seems to imply a spiritual bond that is established between a borrower-lender as the two parties are joined together in relationship.

For more than twenty years I have been asking people the following question:

"If you had no debt payments to make, would your finances be sufficient for you to live on?"

For more than 20 years the answer has been the same: "If I had no debt, sure I would have enough...I would have plenty."—Then ***debt*** is the problem.

> **How long have credit cards been around?**
>
> **According to the Encyclopedia Britannica, the use of credit cards originated in the U.S. during the 1920s, when individual companies, such as hotel chains and oil companies, began issuing them to customers for purchases made at their businesses. This use increased significantly after World War II.**

Habakkuk 2:6-7 (NASB)

6 Will not all of these take up a taunt-song against him, even mockery and insinuations against him and say, 'Woe to him who increases what is not his—for how long—and makes himself rich with loans?' 7 Will not your creditors rise up suddenly, and those who collect from you awaken? Indeed, you will become plunder for them.

Borrowing has become a way of life

We have been taught to buy now and pay later—the catch is that you still have to pay it back but with interest.

Example: Assume you buy something on credit for $1,000. Assuming monthly payments of $50; It will take you two years or 24 months to pay it off and cost you $1200, interest included (most consumer debt carries 15% to 21% interest). In addition, you will have to earn approximately $1700, and then pay income tax, to have $1200 left over to pay off the debt.

Slogans of our time

- Buy Now, Pay Later!
- Instant Credit Approval!
- Easy Payments!

- Make No Payments Until 20..(next year) or even 20..(the following year)!!
- Choose the ANY COMPANY "No Hassle" Card
- Zero % Interest on Balance Transfers for Life
- The Card that Pays You Back
- It's Everywhere You Want to Be
- Save 10% on your Purchase today with an ANY COMPANY Card!
- Priceless

Many people are enticed by these so called deals. However, if you read the fine print, you will realize that you must follow some very specific rules. If you do not, the penalty can be extreme.

How have you been affected by the slogans of our times?

____

____

____

____

____

____

____

People take on debt thinking that their income will increase to cover payments. However, the average income after inflation is actually going down.

Overspending has become a problem as pervasive as over eating!

Consider the consequences of overspending $100 per month (or $3.29 per day). Assume a credit card rate of 19% compounded monthly for 20 years.

This illustration will show you how a little careless overspending can wreck your family's finances and rob you of your freedom. Just think what overspending in larger amounts, or binge spending, will do to financial freedom.

Year	Amount Overspent	Accumulated Interest	End of Year Balance
1	$1,200	$110.21	$1,310.21
2	$1,200	$382.01	$2,892.22
3	$1,200	$710.20	$4,802.42
4	$1,200	$1,106.48	$7,108.90
5	$1,200	$1,584.96	$9,893.86
6	$1,200	$2,162.71	$13,256.57
7	$1,200	$2,860.31	$17,316.88
8	$1,200	$3,702.62	$22,219.50
9	$1,200	$4,719.67	$28,139.17
10	$1,200	$5,947.72	$35,286.89
11	$1,200	$7,430.53	$43,917.42
12	$1,200	$9,220.92	$54,338.34
13	$1,200	$11,382.76	$66,921.10
14	$1,200	$13,993.06	$82,114.16
15	$1,200	$17,144.88	$110,459.04
16	$1,200	$20,950.54	$122,609.58
17	$1,200	$25,545.69	$149,355.27
18	$1,200	$31,094.11	$181,649.38
19	$1,200	$37,793.59	$220,642.97
20	$1,200	$45,882.82	$267,725.79
Total	**$24,000**	**$243,725.79**	**$267,725.79**

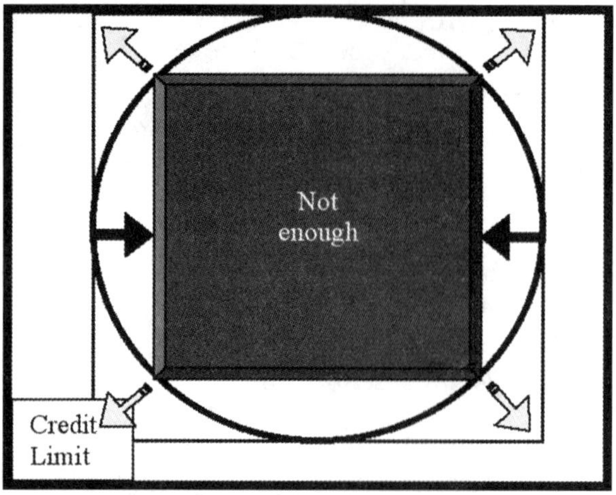

The circle represents our net income: For example $3,000 income per month, but spending $3,500 per month until credit limit is reached (large square).

Assume cost of household is $2,700 per month. Ultimate consequence- $800 payments and living on $2,200 per month. Shortfall of $500 is now covered by credit card leading to ultimate disaster.

Do you see the cycle?

Debt is a symptom of other underlying problems

The underlying root causes are usually one or more of the following:

- Greed
- Lack of Contentment
- Lack of Self-discipline
- Impatience
- Poor self-image

What are the underlying causes for buying on credit in your life?

____

____

____

____

____

____

____

The underlying cause could be a spiritual consequence

Consider the following verses:

Malachi 3:8-11 (NLT)

[8]"Should people cheat God? Yet you have cheated Me! But you ask, 'What do you mean? When did we ever cheat you?'"

"You have cheated Me of the tithes and offerings due to Me. [9]You are under a curse, for your whole nation has been cheating Me. [10]Bring all the tithes into the storehouse so there will be enough food in My Temple. If you do," says the LORD Almighty, "I will open the windows of heaven for you. I will pour out a blessing so great you won't have enough room to take it in! Try it! Let me prove it to you! [11]Your crops will be abundant, for I will guard them from insects and disease. Your grapes will not shrivel before they are ripe," says the LORD Almighty.

Tithing = Blessing

Not Tithing = Curse

Deuteronomy 15:6 (NLT)

[6]The LORD your God will bless you as He has promised. You will lend money to many nations but will never need to borrow! You will rule many nations, but they will not rule over you!

Deuteronomy 28:12 (NLT)

[12]The LORD will send rain at the proper time from his rich treasury in the heavens to bless all the work you do. You will lend to many nations, but you will never need to borrow from them.

His Blessing is that you will lend to many nations, *but you will not need to borrow.*

When we accept God's blessings, then there is no need to borrow because He promises to supply all our needs.

When we don't believe in the blessings God promises in His Word, then we choose to operate under the curse by borrowing.

Deuteronomy 28:44 (Paraphrase)

Curses *are that he (the unbeliever) will lend to you (that means you borrow), and he will become the head and you will become the tail.*

> **For a more thorough review of blessings read Deuteronomy 28:1-14. And for curses read Deuteronomy 28: 15-68.**

Proverbs 22:7 (NLT)

[7]Just as the rich rule the poor, so the borrower is servant to the lender

Once you discover the reason(s) why you take on debt, you can ask the Lord to deliver you from that affliction. Then, getting out of debt becomes easier.

Consider your ways!!

Haggai 1:5-11 (NLT)

[5]This is what the LORD Almighty says: Consider how things are

going for you! [6]You have planted much but harvested little. You have food to eat, but not enough to fill you up. You have wine to drink, but not enough to satisfy your thirst. You have clothing to wear, but not enough to keep you warm. Your wages disappear as though you were putting them in pockets filled with holes!

[7]This is what the LORD Almighty says: Consider how things are going for you! [8]Now go up into the hills, bring down timber, and rebuild My house. Then I will take pleasure in it and be honored, says the LORD. [9]You hoped for rich harvests, but they were poor. And when you brought your harvest home, I blew it away. Why? Because My house lies in ruins, says the LORD Almighty, while you are all busy building your own fine houses. [10]That is why the heavens have withheld the dew and the earth has withheld its crops. [11]I have called for a drought on your fields and hills—a drought to wither the grain and grapes and olives and all your other crops, a drought to starve both you and your cattle and to ruin everything you have worked so hard to get.

Haggai 2:4-9 (NLT)

[4]But now take courage, Zerubbabel, says the LORD. Take courage, Jeshua son of Jehozadak, the high priest. Take courage, all you people still left in the land, says the LORD. Take courage and work, for I am with you, says the LORD Almighty. [5]My Spirit remains among you, just as I promised when you came out of Egypt. So do not be afraid.

[6]For this is what the LORD Almighty says: In just a little while I will again shake the heavens and the earth. I will shake the oceans and the dry land, too. [7]I will shake all the nations, and the treasures of all the nations will come to this Temple. I will fill this place with glory, says the LORD Almighty. [8]The silver is mine, and the gold is mine, says the LORD Almighty. [9]The future glory of this Temple will be greater than its past glory, says the LORD Almighty. And in this place I will bring peace. I, the LORD Almighty, have spoken!

Proverbs 14:8 (NLT)

[8]The wise look ahead to see what is coming, but fools deceive themselves.

Choose life and prosperity, not death and adversity!!

Deuteronomy 30:15 (NLT)

15"Now listen! Today I am giving you a choice between prosperity and disaster, between life and death.

Deuteronomy 30:15 (NASB)

15See, I have set before you today life and prosperity, and death and adversity;

Debt = Bondage
No Debt = Freedom

What does God say about debt?

Consequences of borrowing—the borrower becomes the lender's slave.

Proverbs 22:7 (NASB)

7The rich rules over the poor, And the borrower becomes the lender's slave.

Romans 8:13 (NKJV)

13For if you live according to the flesh you will die; but if by the Spirit you put to death the deeds of the body, you will live.

Numbers 30:2 (NASB)

2"If a man makes a vow to the LORD, or takes an oath to bind himself with a binding obligation, he shall not violate his word; he shall do according to all that proceeds out of his mouth.

Job 24:9 (NLT)—talks about infants being seized for debt

9"The wicked snatch a widow's child from her breast; they take the baby as a pledge for a loan.

2 Kings 4:1 (NLT)

[1]One day the widow of one of Elisha's fellow prophets came to Elisha and cried out to him, "My husband who served you is dead, and you know how he feared the LORD. But now a creditor has come, threatening to take my two sons as slaves."

> **Take some time to read the rest of the story recorded in 2 Kings 4. It is a great story of faith.**

Luke 16:13 (The Message)

No worker can serve two bosses: He'll either hate the first and love the second, Or adore the first and despise the second.

You can't serve both God and the Bank.

Deuteronomy 6:13-15 (NLT)

[13]You must fear the LORD your God and serve him. When you take an oath, you must use only His name.[14]"You must not worship any of the gods of neighboring nations, [15]for the LORD your God, who lives among you, is a jealous God. His anger will flare up against you and wipe you from the face of the earth.

Luke 14:28-30 (NLT)

[28]But don't begin until you count the cost. For who would begin construction of a building without first getting estimates and then checking to see if there is enough money to pay the bills?
[29]Otherwise, you might complete only the foundation before running out of funds. And then how everyone would laugh at
you! [30]They would say, "There's the person who started that building and ran out of money before it was finished!"

James 4:3 (NLT)

[3]And even when you do ask, you don't get it because your whole motive is wrong—you want only what will give you pleasure.

Meditate on James 4:3 and write your thoughts

____

____

____

____

____

____

____

____

The real world—consequences of taking on debt

- We think we need things right now.
- We are not patient enough to wait upon the Lord.
- We buy on credit and then pray for the payments

Our debt keeps us on a treadmill and robs us of our seed!

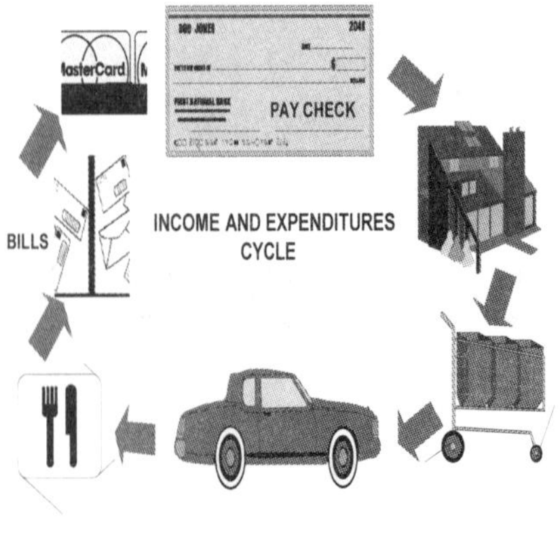

Reflect on what you have learned so far. What is your view of debt? Do you consider debt to be bondage?

____

____

____

____

____

____

____

Before purchasing, ask yourself: Is this something I really need or something I really want?

Make a commitment to tithe and there will be no need to borrow

2 Chronicles 31:10 (NASB)

[10]Azariah the chief priest of the house of Zadok said to him, "Since the contributions began to be brought into the house of the LORD, we have had enough to eat with plenty left over, for the LORD has blessed His people, and this great quantity is left over."

On cosigning—don't!

Proverbs 17:18 (NLT)

[18]It is poor judgment to co-sign a friend's note, to become responsible for a neighbor's debts.

Proverbs 22:26-27 (NLT)

[26]Do not co-sign another person's note or put up a guarantee for someone else's loan. [27]If you can't pay it, even your bed will be snatched from under you.

Have you ever cosigned for someone?
How did it turn out?

____

____

____

____

____

____

____

____

If you have already cosigned, pray about the situation, and then remove yourself from the liability as soon as possible.

Proverbs 6:1-5 (NLT)

[1]My child, if you co-sign a loan for a friend or guarantee the debt of someone you hardly know—[2]if you have trapped yourself by your agreement and are caught by what you said—[3]quick, get out of it if you possibly can! You have placed yourself at your friend's mercy. Now swallow your pride; go and beg to have your name erased. [4]Don't put it off. Do it now! Don't rest until you do. [5]Save yourself like a deer escaping from a hunter, like a bird fleeing from a net.

Proverbs 11:15 (NLT)

[15]Guaranteeing a loan for a stranger is dangerous; it is better to refuse than to suffer later.

On Auto Loans

If you buy a new $18,000 car every four years with 10% down, 4% interest and 48 months to pay, the total cost of ownership will be $42,957.

Year	1	2	3	4
Gasoline	$1,200	$1,200	$1,200	$1,200
Oil Change	$120	$120	$120	$120
Maintenance	$0	$0	$0	$150
Repairs	$0	$0	$0	$350
License	$360	$270	$200	$177
Sales Tax 7.5%	$1,350	$0	$0	$0
Insurance	$950	$950	$950	$950
Loan Payment	$4,390	$4,390	$4,390	$4,390
Down Payment	$1,800	$0	$0	$0
Depreciation	$4,500	$3,500	$2,500	$1,150
Cost Per Year	$14,671	$10,432	$9,363	$8,491

If you buy the same car three-years-old, it would cost $7,500 in cash. The total cost of ownership will be $24,313.

Year	1	2	3	4
Gasoline	$1,200	$1,200	$1,200	$1,200
Oil Change	$120	$120	$120	$120
Maintenance	$250	$270	$300	$320
Repairs	$350	$500	$600	$700
License	$150	$130	$110	$90
Sales Tax 7.5%	$563	$0	$0	$0
Insurance	$800	$800	$800	$800
Loan Payment	$0	$0	$0	$0
Down Payment	$7,500	$0	$0	$0
Depreciation	$1,000	$1,000	$1,000	$1,000
Cost Per Year	$11,933	$4,020	$4,130	$4,230

Four Year Cost of Ownership:

New Car	$42,957
Used Car	$24,313
Savings	$18,644

What alternatives to buying on credit can you think of?

____

____

____

____

____

____

____

On installment loans

Installment Loans are usually short-term loans of 3 to 5 years in duration.

Consider your choices for a $20,000 loan at 9.5% interest. If you select a five year loan, you will pay $420 per month and $5,200 interest over the life of the loan. Your total cash payments are $25,200. If you choose a three year loan instead, your payments rise to about $640 per month. Total interest over the life of the loan is $3,060 making your total cash payments $23,060.

On mortgages

There are a variety of mortgage loan arrangements available today (i.e. fixed, variable, 30-year, 15-year, etc.).

The cost of mortgage payments and related tax savings for mortgage interest deductions is often close to actual rent payments. There are advantages and disadvantages to owning a home vs. renting a home.

Let's take a look...

Some Advantages of Home Ownership

- ❋ Home ownership gives a sense of belonging and security
- ❋ Home ownership establishes a credit rating
- ❋ Home ownership can generate a sense of enjoyment and satisfaction
- ❋ If you have a fixed interest rate, your payments stay the same over the long-term
- ❋ Home ownership can create a valuable asset
- ❋ Tax savings for mortgage interest deductions

Some Disadvantages of Home Ownership

- ❋ The homeowner must assume responsibility for financing, maintenance, care and improvements; renters on the other hand leave those responsibilities to the landlord
- ❋ Home ownership may require larger monthly expenditures compared to renting when you consider upkeep, improvements, taxes and insurance
- ❋ Real estate is subject to price fluctuations. The current cost may not be indicative of its future value.

The average length of time for home ownership before the property is sold or refinanced is 5 to 7 years. When you consider a $200,000 loan at 6% in the first 5 years you pay principal and interest of $1,991.10 per month. The bank loans you the $200,000 and they collect all of it back plus $58,054.80 in interest. You assume all the risk of gain or loss on the sale of the property. Plus, you pay all insurance, taxes, and upkeep during the 5 years. History would show that in the past, values increased far more than the cost of ownership.

On Refinancing – a slippery slope!

It helps you temporarily to take the pressure off, but most of the time you are only digging a deeper hole.

Refinancing often turns out to be a quick fix. In six months to two years you are in trouble again. When you do this, you are actually spending your equity until there is nothing left.

Only when you have learned *why* you live beyond your means and have made a commitment to change your ways and get out of debt, only then is refinancing an option to reduce the interest rate.

Chapter synthesis

In this chapter we learned that debt is bondage. God does not want us in debt. As a matter of fact, He warns us about getting into debt. It is interesting to see that His Word tells us that if we tithe, we are under the blessing and we will not borrow. But if we do not tithe, we come under the curse and we will borrow and eventually become the lender's slave.

Notes and reflections...

Chapter 8: Debt—How to Eliminate It

In This Chapter

- Debt-free living
- Getting debt under control
- Making the commitment not to borrow again
- Turning your debts over to God
- Taking responsibility
- Selling what you don't need
- A plan for getting out of debt

Debt-free living—it seems far fetched; even impossible. But "with God all things are possible." (Matt. 19:26 NIV) You *can* be financially free, the chains of bondage *can* be broken, and you *can* take your rightful place as a child of God as the head and not the tail. In the last chapter we talked about how DEBT is THE problem with our finances. God has the answers. Let's now take a look at the solutions from His Kingdom perspective...

As long as we accept debt as a way of life, we are deceived and remain in bondage. Often we think that if we had just a little more money, we could make it. That is a lie.

Listen to this closely: *until you stop borrowing, you are not yet committed to getting out of debt.*

Beware of ever thinking, "Oh, that thing in my life doesn't matter much." The fact that it doesn't matter much to you may mean that it matters a great deal to God.

Do you protest that your heart is right with God, and yet there is something in your life He causes you to doubt? Whenever God causes a doubt about something, stop it immediately, no matter what it may be. Nothing in our lives is a mere insignificant detail to God.

Oswald Chambers *My Utmost for His Highest*

How to get debt under control and how to get out from under it?

1. Confess your transgressions
2. Make a commitment not to borrow again
3. Turn your debts over to God (but take responsibility)
4. Sell what you don't need
5. Do not withhold repayment

Confess your transgressions

As long as we are in debt we are in bondage. There is a spiritual bondage which takes place between the one who lends and the one who borrows.

Proverbs 22:7 (The Message)

The poor are always ruled over by the rich, so don't borrow and put yourself under their power.

Proverbs 28:13 (NLT)

[13]People who cover over their sins will not prosper. But if they confess and forsake them, they will receive mercy.

Food for thought:

The Hebrew word for "borrow" or "lend" in the Old Testament is also at times translated—"to join with" or "attached to". This seems to imply a spiritual bond that is established between a borrower-lender as the two parties are joined together in relationship.

We have to break the spiritual bondage between us and the lender. Since the spiritual realm precedes the physical manifestation, we need to ask God to let His *unconditional* forgiveness flow through our hearts to forgive and release the lender. Then we need to ask God to let His unconditional forgiveness flow through the heart of the lender and ask for the lender to forgive and release us. When the spiritual bondage is broken, the physical will manifest itself.

Matthew 6:14-15 (The Message)

In prayer there is a connection between what God does and what you do. You can't get forgiveness from God, for instance, without also forgiving others. If you refuse to do your part, you cut yourself off from God's part.

Matthew 6:12 (NKJV)

[12]And forgive us our debts, As we forgive our debtors.

Matthew 18:27 (NASB)

[27]"And the lord of that slave felt compassion and released him and forgave him the debt.

2 Corinthians 2:10 (NLT) Paul speaking

[10]When you forgive this man, I forgive him, too. And when I forgive him (for whatever is to be forgiven), I do so with Christ's authority for your benefit.

Who are your creditors? Have you forgiven them?

____

____

____

____

____

____

____

____

Ephesians 4:32 (NASB)

32 Be kind to one another, tender-hearted, forgiving each other, just as God in Christ also has forgiven you.

1 John 1:9 (NKJV)

9 If we confess our sins, He is faithful and just to forgive us our sins and to cleanse us from all unrighteousness.

Matthew 16:19 (NASB)

19 I will give you the keys of the kingdom of heaven; and whatever you bind on earth shall have been bound in heaven, and whatever you loose on earth shall have been loosed in heaven.

Psalm 116:16 (NLT)

16 O LORD, I am your servant; yes, I am your servant, the son of your handmaid, and you have freed me from my bonds!

Romans 7:6 (NASB)

6But now we have been released from the Law, having died to that by which we were bound, so that we serve in newness of the Spirit and not in oldness of the letter.

Make a commitment not to borrow again

As soon as you make a commitment to get out of debt and not to borrow again (REPENT), you will feel a freedom and peace that is difficult to describe.

Satan does not want to see God glorified in your life, neither to have freedom and peace, so he will put pressure on you to stay in debt or get back in debt. The best way to keep the pressure off is to systematically pay off all old obligations and trust God to supply all your needs.

Although you have made a commitment to get out of debt, it will only be meaningful if you agree not to borrow again. If you are looking for God to bail you out and immediately borrow again, it will not work. God knows the intentions of your heart.

A *true* commitment leaves no other option!

Galatians 6:7 (NASB)

7Do not be deceived, God is not mocked; for whatever a man sows, this he will also reap.

Borrowing can be avoided if you plan ahead

(Luke 14:28-30 NASB)

28For which one of you, when he wants to build a tower, does not first sit down and calculate the cost to see if he has enough to complete it? 29Otherwise, when he has laid a foundation and is not able to finish, all who observe it begin to ridicule him, 30saying, 'This man began to build and was not able to finish.'

We have all done it. Can you remember a time when you had to spend more than you had intended, simply because you did not plan ahead? What was the outcome?

Questions to reflect upon: Have you studied the scriptures that warn you about being in debt (Chapter 7)? Why are you committed to getting out of debt? Remember: a true commitment leaves no other option.

Can you agree not to borrow again, no matter what?

Do you understand that cosigning, in principal, is the same as borrowing?

Turn your debts over to God (but take responsibility)

Trust in the Lord with all your heart

Proverbs 3:5-6 (NASB)

5 *Trust in the LORD with all your heart And do not lean on your*

own understanding.[6]In all your ways acknowledge Him, And He will make your paths straight.

Hebrews 6:12 (NLT)

[12]Then you will not become spiritually dull and indifferent. Instead, you will follow the example of those who are going to inherit God's promises because of their faith and patience.

Call upon Him for help and strength

Psalm 50:15 (NKJV)

[15]Call upon Me in the day of trouble, I will deliver you, and you shall glorify Me.

Psalm 37:5 (NKJV)

[5]Commit your way to the LORD, Trust also in Him, And He shall bring it to pass.

Why do you think it is important to take full responsibility for your debts?

____

____

____

____

____

____

____

____

____

Ecclesiastes 7:14 (The Message)

On a good day, enjoy yourself; On a bad day, examine your conscience. God arranges for both kinds of days So that we won't take anything for granted.

What evidence do you see of God moving and arranging the days of your life?

____

____

____

____

____

____

____

____

Take responsibility

A plan to become debt free would include a program to pay off existing debt.

Numbers 30:2 (NASB)

2"If a man makes a vow to the LORD, or takes an oath to bind himself with a binding obligation, he shall not violate his word; he shall do according to all that proceeds out of his mouth.

Matthew 18:19-20 (NLT)

19"I also tell you this: If two of you agree down here on earth concerning anything you ask, my Father in heaven will do it for you. 20For where two or three gather together because they are mine, I am there among them."

2 Corinthians 9:8 (NLT)

8And God will generously provide all you need. Then you will always have everything you need and plenty left over to share with others.

Prayer for financial freedom

Heavenly Father,

I come before You today in the Name of Your Son, Jesus. I know that I am cleansed through His blood. So I stand before You perfect in Your Son, complete, lacking in nothing.

Father God, I confess that I have made many mistakes financially and as a result, I am in bondage with many people and creditors. So today, I turn over the entire mess, just as You instructed me to do. I commit unto You all of my belongings, my assets, my liabilities, my income and my expenses. They are Yours. I trust You completely. I know You will take care of all of my needs from this point forward. Please guide me and direct me in everything I do, everything I speak and in every step I take. From this day forward I am working for You, under Your guidance and direction. My aim is to do everything unto You, to please You and to assist others in everything I undertake.

Lord God, I now bring Your words with me, as I pray to be freed from the bondage of finance so I can serve You. Your Word says that whatever I bind on earth shall be bound in heaven and whatever I loose on earth shall be loosed in heaven. Spirit of GREED, spirit of WANT, spirit of IDOLATRY and spirit of COVETOUSNESS, I come against you in the Name of Jesus. I rebuke you in the Name of Jesus. I bind you with the blood of Jesus and command you IN HIS NAME to return to the darkness where you came from. I also come against the spirit of DEBT in the NAME OF JESUS. I rebuke you in the Name of Jesus and bind you with His blood. IN HIS NAME, I release you from your assignment against me and render you totally powerless. It is written that you spirits of darkness were defeated by Jesus a long time ago and no longer have any say in my life. Now, to fill the vacant places in my heart, I release the spirit of LOVE, WISDOM, GRATEFULNESS, CONTENTMENT, TITHING and GIVING. I embrace those godly gifts to my heart to guide me and direct me in every decision I make and every step I take. I thank You, Father in Jesus' Name.

Father God, I now would like Your help in setting me free from the financial bondage of all my creditors. I have listed each and every name of my creditors. In Jesus' Name I ask that

You now flow Your unconditional FORGIVENESS from Your throne in heaven and cleanse my heart as I fully FORGIVE and RELEASE ________.

I also ask that You flow Your unconditional FORGIVENESS and RELEASE from Your throne in heaven and cleanse ______ heart, as he completely forgives and releases me. We are both free and no longer encumbered spiritually. (Repeat for each and every creditor).

Thank You Father God, in Jesus' Name, for setting me completely free!!!

Now make a commitment to pay back every obligation as quickly as possible.

Sell what you do not need

Sell those things which you do not need and apply the proceeds toward your debts. Liquidate investments and apply the proceeds toward your debts. Remember: your best investment… is your debt!

Example: The bank is paying you, let's say 4% interest on your savings account; the same bank is charging you 18% interest on your credit card. If you take from your savings to pay off the credit card debt, you are earning 18% on your money.

First, consider what the pressure of your debt feels like. Then imagine what the freedom will feel like when you have paid off your debt. Write down those thoughts here.

____

____

____

____

____

Do not withhold repayment

Proverbs 3:27-28 (TLB)—see also NKJV

[27-28]Don't withhold repayment of your debts. Don't say "some other time," if you can pay now.

2 Kings 4:1-7 (NASB)

[1]Now a certain woman of the wives of the sons of the prophets cried out to Elisha, "Your servant my husband is dead, and you know that your servant feared the LORD; and the creditor has come to take my two children to be his slaves." [2]Elisha said to her, "What shall I do for you? Tell me, what do you have in the house?" And she said, "Your maidservant has nothing in the house except a jar of oil." [3]Then he said, "Go, borrow vessels at large for yourself from all your neighbors, even empty vessels; do not get a few. [4]And you shall go in and shut the door behind you and your sons, and pour out into all these vessels, and you shall set aside what is full." [5]So she went from him and shut the door behind her and her sons; they were bringing the vessels to her and she poured. [6]When the vessels were full, she said to her son, "Bring me another vessel." And he said to her, "There is not one vessel more." And the oil stopped. [7]Then she came and told the man of God. And he said, "Go, sell the oil and pay your debt, and you and your sons can live on the rest."

Proverbs 21:20 (NASB)

[20]There is precious treasure and oil in the dwelling of the wise, But a foolish man swallows it up.

Matthew 18:23-27 (NKJV)

[2]Therefore the kingdom of heaven is like a certain king who wanted to settle accounts with his servants. [24]And when he had begun to settle accounts, one was brought to him who owed him ten thousand talents. [25]But as he was not able to pay, his master commanded that he be sold, with his wife and children and all that he had, and that payment be made. [26]The servant therefore fell down before him, saying, 'Master, have patience with me, and I will pay you all.' [27]Then the master of that servant was moved with compassion, released him, and forgave him the debt.

Notice that:

- The servant *confirmed* the debt
- He promised to pay it back
- The king forgave the debt

How do these verses apply to your own situation?

____

____

____

____

____

____

____

____

A plan for getting out of debt

Ask yourself how long it will take to get caught up and get out of debt. The answer is usually five to seven years, but often even much longer. Unless we change our ways, there is no way of getting out of debt. *The system is designed to keep you in it.*

But—whom do you believe? God's Word says that Christ came to set you free. (Galatians 5:1)

Step 1: Make a commitment to get out of debt

Remember—a true *commitment* leaves no other option!

Step 2: Make a commitment not to borrow again, no matter what

Step 3: Prioritize your spending

1. First, pay your tithe
2. Second, pay your taxes
3. Third, meet the needs of your household (that requires a budget)
4. Fourth, apply the rest toward your debt (you should be out of debt within six months to two years)

But remember—***Stop Borrowing***—-it is not an option.

Make extra payments as often as you can

A plan to become debt free would include a program to pay off existing debt. Remember it took us years to get into the situation we are in, so it will take some time to get our situation back in order. When making extra payments on debt, it is wise to reduce debt which bears the highest interest rate first. When an account is paid off, then shift that payment and the extra payment to another account until they are all paid off.

Face the facts

List your debts, balance, monthly payments, and interest rates. Ask God to give you wisdom to use your talents to earn extra income to apply toward existing debts.

Reduce your standard of living to allow the maximum to be applied toward reducing your debt. Sacrifice a little and get out of debt a lot faster.

Ask God to give you creative ways to sell what you do not need and apply the proceeds toward you debt.

Examples of extra payments

Early Pay-off of a home mortgage:

Facts- $175,000 Mortgage @ 7% over 30 years (360 months) = $1,165.23/month

Regular Payment	Extra Payment	Total Payment	Months to Pay-off	$ Savings	Payments Saved
$1,165.23	---	$1,165.23	360	---	---
$1,165.23	$10.00	$1,175.23	350	$11,652.30	10 Months
$1,165.23	$25.00	$1,190.23	336	$27,965.52	2 Years
$1,165.23	$50.00	$1,215.23	315	$52,435.35	3 Yrs 9 Mos
$1,165.23	$100.00	$1,265.23	283	$89,722.71	6 Yrs 5 Mos

Facts- $175,000 Mortgage @ 7% over 15 years (180 months) = $1,572.95/month

Regular Payment	Extra Payment	Total Payment	Months to Pay-off	$ Savings	Payments Saved
$1,572.95	—	$1,572.95	180	—	—
$1,572.95	$10.00	$1,582.95	178	$3,145.90	2 Months
$1,572.95	$25.00	$1,597.95	175	$7,864.60	5 Months
$1,572.95	$50.00	$1,622.95	170	$15,729.50	10 Months
$1,572.95	$100.00	$1,672.95	161	$29,886.05	1 Yr 7 Mos

Alternatives to purchasing a car on credit:

Historical way of buying a car

- **Buy car for $15,000**
- **Trade-in old car**
- **48 payments of $400/month**

RESULT – In 4 years you are driving an "old" car and need to buy a new one.

Recommended way of buying a car

- **Save $400 for six months**
- **Trade Old Car in (Trade Up) with $2,400 Cash**
- **Save $400/month for six months (or more)**
- **Trade up with cash**

Result—in less than four years you will be driving a "new car"—*paid in full*!

Chapter synthesis

In this chapter we learned that it is possible to get out of debt. When we follow God's Word and instructions we can learn how to eliminate debt and how to stay out of it. After all, it was Jesus who set us free. Since He set us free, why on earth do we choose to become slaves to the lender?

Notes and reflections…

Chapter 9: Tithing and Giving

In This Chapter

- Tithing
- Do churches need to tithe?
- Tithing on the gross or the net?
- Where to take the tithe
- Giving
- What are alms?

God wants us to give tithes and offerings to Him. When we tithe we acknowledge that God is our source and that our earnings are a gift from Him. A tithe is a tenth of one's income. God's Word says that if we do not tithe we are withholding that which is due God, and we are actually robbing Him. When we choose not to tithe, we are subject to the curses for disobedience. They are fully discussed in Deuteronomy 28:15-68. Among those curses is the statement that we shall borrow, as discussed in the previous chapter on debt. When we choose to be obedient to

His Word and tithe, we shall be blessed. The blessings are also discussed in Deuteronomy 28:1-14. Among those blessings is the statement that we shall not borrow. These verses suggest that borrowing is a symptom of financial *bondage*, and that the actual causes of financial bondage begin as a result of not tithing.

The Bible tells us that we should not put the Lord to test, except in the area of tithing. We are to bring the whole tithe, not part of it. Then God will rebuke Satan for us. *When we are tithing, and Satan comes against us, we need to resist him by asking the Father to rebuke him. Satan will flee when the Father comes after him.* We should not rationalize why it would be all right to give less than the whole tithe.

We also need to evaluate our giving program. We should first of all make a commitment to give. Then we need to ask God to guide us as to when, where, and how much to give, over and above the tithe. We are stewards of that which God has entrusted to us.

What we sow is what we reap. When our tithes are sown in good soil, they will bear fruit—thirty, sixty, and a hundredfold. Jesus said that when we let go of the things of the world for His sake or for the Gospel's sake, we shall receive one hundred times as much as we give up. When we give more, we get more in return. This is what is promised in His Word.

Tithing

How do you feel about tithing?—search our hearts, oh Lord.

Examine the following scripture called The Parable of the Sower.

Matthew 13:18-23 (NLT)

18Now here is the explanation of the story I told about the farmer
sowing grain: 19The seed that fell on the hard path represents
those who hear the Good News about the Kingdom and don't
understand it. Then the evil one comes and snatches the seed
away from their hearts. 20The rocky soil represents those who
hear the message and receive it with joy. 21But like young plants

in such soil, their roots don't go very deep. At first they get along fine, but they wilt as soon as they have problems or are persecuted because they believe the Word. [22]The thorny ground represents those who hear and accept the Good News, but all too quickly the message is crowded out by the cares of this life and the lure of wealth, so no crop is produced. [23]The good soil represents the hearts of those who truly accept God's message and produce a huge harvest—thirty, sixty, or even a hundred times as much as had been planted.

There are 4 types of soil mentioned:

1. Hard soil
2. Rocky soil
3. Thorny soil
4. Good soil

What condition is your heart in?

Oftentimes when it comes to reading or hearing scriptures about tithing and giving, we are not prepared to receive the Word. There is a tendency to rationalize and come up with all kinds of excuses why we don't have to tithe.

Some Christians say that tithing is an Old Testament law which no longer applies to believers today. But remember that Jesus said in Matthew 5 that He did not come to abolish the Law but to fulfill it.

Take some time to search your heart and be honest with the Lord. How do you really feel about tithing?

____

____

____

____

____

____

____

Tithing is an untouched issue in some churches. Why? Because it is a topic that many people are uncomfortable with. The better question to ask might be: Lord, how do You feel about tithing? Let's take a look at the Word to see what it has to say.

Malachi 3:8-12 (NKJV)

8 Will a man rob God? Yet you have robbed Me! But you say, "In what way have we robbed You?" In tithes and offerings. 9 You are cursed with a curse, For you have robbed Me, Even this whole nation. 10 Bring all the tithes into the storehouse, That there may be food in My house, And try Me now in this," Says the LORD of hosts, If I will not open for you the windows of heaven And pour out for you such blessing That there will not be room enough to receive it. 11 And I will rebuke the devourer for your sakes, So that he will not destroy the fruit of your ground, Nor shall the vine fail to bear fruit for you in the field, Says the LORD of hosts; 12 And all nations will call you blessed, For you will be a delightful land, Says the LORD of hosts.

The Lord challenges us to *test* Him! Have you ever tried it?

Genesis 4:3-5 (NLT)

[3]At harvest time Cain brought to the LORD a gift of his farm produce, [4]while Abel brought several choice lambs from the best of his flock. The LORD accepted Abel and his offering, [5]but he did not accept Cain and his offering. This made Cain very angry and dejected.

Tithing began in the earliest stages of Genesis. Abel gave from his best. Cain did not.

Hebrews 11:4 (NASB)

[4]By faith Abel offered to God a better sacrifice than Cain, through which he obtained the testimony that he was righteous, God testifying about his gifts, and through faith, though he is dead, he still speaks.

Genesis 14:20 (b) (NLT)

Then Abram gave Melchizedek a tenth of all the goods he had recovered.

Deuteronomy 14:22 (NASB)

[22]You shall surely tithe all the produce from what you sow, which comes out of the field every year.

Proverbs 11:24 (NLT)

[24]It is possible to give freely and become more wealthy, but those who are stingy will lose everything.

It is interesting how we often justify ourselves. Often people say, "I wish I had some left-over to tithe to the Lord." *The Lord does not want leftovers.* The tithe is the *first* of all our produce. The first is *always* there to give.

Leviticus 27:30 (NKJV)

[30]And all the tithe of the land, whether of the seed of the land or of the fruit of the tree, is the LORD's. It is holy to the LORD.

Leviticus 27:32 (NKJV)

[32]And concerning the tithe of the herd or the flock, of whatever passes under the rod, the tenth one shall be holy to the LORD.

What does the word *holy* mean? Some scholars have defined it as "Set apart for God's use."

Why can you trust God to use the money you give?

Establish a Tithing Program

I cannot stress enough how very important it is to set and reach a goal of tithing 10%. You must establish a tithing program in your family. Unless you tithe, you can never walk in financial freedom because you are robbing God. If you are having a particularly hard time trusting God to meet your needs when you tithe, start out with 5% and work your way up to 10% over a six month period of time. Test Him.

Do Churches need to tithe?

A church sets the example for the members.

Numbers 18:25-26 (NLT)

25 The LORD also told Moses, 26 Say this to the Levites: "When you receive the tithes from the Israelites, give a tenth of the tithes you receive—a tithe of the tithe—to the LORD as a gift."

Nehemiah 10:38 (NLT)

38 A priest—a descendant of Aaron—will be with the Levites as they receive these tithes. And a tenth of all that is collected as tithes will be delivered by the Levites to the Temple of our God and placed in the storerooms.

Most churches tithe on a regular basis to mission organizations or outreach projects in the community. Get involved in these projects with your family. What a lesson in authentic Christianity for you and your children!

Should I tithe on the gross or on the net?

The Bible is clear that the "firstfruits" are to be given. It also depends on whether you want Him to bless you on the gross or the net.

2 Chronicles 31:5 (NLT)

[5]The people responded immediately and generously with the first of their crops and grain, new wine, olive oil, honey, and all the produce of their fields. They brought a tithe of all they owned.

Try this: the next time you get your paycheck, thank the Lord for it, and before you have deposited it write your tithe check for the amount you have prayed about ahead of time with your spouse. By giving it to the Lord right away, you will feel less inclined to count that money as your own. All of it belongs to Him anyway.

Nehemiah 10:34-39 (NLT)

[34]We have cast sacred lots to determine when—at regular times each year—the families of the priests, Levites, and the common people should bring wood to God's Temple to be burned on the altar of the LORD our God, as required in the law.

[35]We promise always to bring the first part of every harvest to
the LORD'S Temple—whether it be a crop from the soil or from
our fruit trees. [36]We agree to give to God our oldest sons and the
firstborn of all our herds and flocks, just as the law requires.
We will present them to the priests who minister in the Temple
of our God. [37]We will store the produce in the storerooms of the
Temple of our God. We will bring the best of our flour and other
grain offerings, the best of our fruit, and the best of our new wine
and olive oil. And we promise to bring to the Levites a tenth of
everything our land produces, for it is the Levites who collect
the tithes in all our rural towns. [38]A priest—a descendant of
Aaron—will be with the Levites as they receive these tithes. And

a tenth of all that is collected as tithes will be delivered by the Levites to the Temple of our God and placed in the storerooms. [39]The people and the Levites must bring these offerings of grain, new wine, and olive oil to the Temple and place them in the sacred containers near the ministering priests, the gatekeepers, and the singers.

So we promise together not to neglect the Temple of our God.

Proverbs 3:9 (NLT)

[9]Honor the LORD with your wealth and with the best part of everything your land produces.

Where do you take the tithe?

The tithe should be taken to your church.

Deuteronomy 26:2 (NLT)

[2]...put some of the first produce from each harvest into a basket and bring it to the place the LORD your God chooses for His Name to be honored.

Nehemiah 10:36 (NLT)

[36]We agree to give to God our oldest sons and the firstborn of all our herds and flocks, just as the law requires. We will present them to the priests who minister in the Temple of our God.

Treasurers or Stewards were in charge of the storehouse.

Nehemiah 13:12-13 (NKJV)

[12]Then all Judah brought the tithe of the grain and the new wine and the oil to the storehouse. [13]And I appointed as treasurers over the storehouse Shelemiah the priest and Zadok the scribe, and of the Levites, Pedaiah; and next to them was Hanan the son of Zaccur, the son of Mattaniah; for they were considered faithful, and their task was to distribute to their brethren.

2 Chronicles 31:4 (NKJV)

[4]Moreover he commanded the people who dwelt in Jerusalem to contribute support for the priests and the Levites, that they might devote themselves to the Law of the LORD.

Luke 8:1-3 (NLT)

[1]Not long afterward Jesus began a tour of the nearby cities and
villages to announce the Good News concerning the Kingdom of
God. He took his twelve disciples with Him, [2]along with some
women He had healed and from whom He had cast out evil
spirits. Among them were Mary Magdalene, from whom He
had cast out seven demons; [3]Joanna, the wife of Chuza, Herod's
business manager; Susanna; and many others who were
contributing from their own resources to support Jesus and His
disciples.

Luke 10:3-7 (NLT)

[3]Go now, and remember that I am sending you out as lambs
among wolves. [4]Don't take along any money, or a traveler's bag,
or even an extra pair of sandals. And don't stop to greet anyone
on the road.

[5]Whenever you enter a home, give it your blessing. [6]If those who
live there are worthy, the blessing will stand; if they are not,
the blessing will return to you. [7]When you enter a town, don't
move around from home to home. Stay in one place, eating
and drinking what they provide you. Don't hesitate to accept
hospitality, because those who work deserve their pay.

1 Corinthians 9:7-8,10(b)-11 & 14 (NLT)

[7]What soldier has to pay his own expenses? And have you ever
heard of a farmer who harvests his crop and doesn't have the
right to eat some of it? What shepherd takes care of a flock of
sheep and isn't allowed to drink some of the milk? [8]And this
isn't merely human opinion. Doesn't God's law say the same
thing?

Christian workers should be paid by those they serve.[11]We have
planted good spiritual seed among you. Is it too much to ask, in
return, for mere food and clothing?

[14]In the same way, the Lord gave orders that those who preach the Good News should be supported by those who benefit from it.

Galatians 6:6 (NLT)

[6]Those who are taught the word of God should help their teachers by paying them.

3 John 1:7-8 (NLT)

[7]For they are traveling for the Lord and accept nothing from those who are not Christians. [8]So we ourselves should support them so that we may become partners with them for the truth.

Why does my attitude in tithing and giving matter?

Attitudes that hinder tithing:

- "I have nothing left over."
- "The church has plenty; they don't need my money."
- "The church does not spend the money as I think they should."

Attitudes that support tithing:

- "I am excited to be a part of His blessing."
- "I do not need to concern myself about the stewardship of others."
- "He has given me so much, and only wants 10% back. Thank you Lord for the 90%."

God wants you to be excited to be a part of His work. If you have a hard time with giving cheerfully, ask God to bless you with a giving heart. And ask Him to reveal to you how He feels when you tithe.

2 Corinthians 9:7 (NLT)

[7]You must each make up your own mind as to how much you should give. Don't give reluctantly or in response to pressure. For God loves the person who gives cheerfully.

The Greek word for cheerful in this passage is "hilaros." From this word, the English word "hilarious" is derived. It is also translated as gracious. So what does that tell about our attitude of giving?

Luke 18:9-14 (NLT)

[9]*Then Jesus told this story to some who had great self-confidence and scorned everyone else:* [10]*"Two men went to the Temple to pray. One was a Pharisee, and the other was a dishonest tax collector.* [11]*The proud Pharisee stood by himself and prayed this prayer: 'I thank You, God, that I am not a sinner like everyone else, especially like that tax collector over there! For I never cheat, I don't sin, I don't commit adultery,* [12]*I fast twice a week, and I give You a tenth of my income.'*

[13]*But the tax collector stood at a distance and dared not even lift his eyes to heaven as he prayed. Instead, he beat his chest in sorrow, saying, 'O God, be merciful to me, for I am a sinner.'* [14]*I tell you, this sinner, not the Pharisee, returned home justified before God. For the proud will be humbled, but the humble will be honored."*

Notice, the Pharisee gave a tenth of his income. Also notice, the condition of his heart compared with the contrite heart of the tax collector.

Consider it a *joy to give to the Kingdom of God.* When you tithe, you are really offering to be a participant in His blessing. The same God who multiplied the loaves and fishes, *will* take whatever you give and *multiply* it in the blessing of His Kingdom.

Don't ever let yourself think that He will benefit more when you save up to build up a bigger tithe.

Don't ever think that your small offering will not be enough to benefit His Kingdom.

In Chapter 4 we pointed out four levels of financial well-being:

- Never having enough
- Having Just enough
- Having more than enough

- Having an abundance to give and bless others

These are attitudes. We have been blessed in this country beyond measure. Most of us have an abundance when we compare ourselves to the rest of the world.

According to **Malachi 3:10 (NASB)**

"Bring the whole tithe into the storehouse, so that there may be food in my house, and test me now in this", says the Lord of hosts, "if I will not open for you the windows of heaven, and pour out for you a blessing until it overflows".

Proverbs 11:24-25 (NLT)

24 *There is one who scatters, yet increases more; And there is one who withholds more than is right, But it leads to poverty.* 25 *The generous soul will be made rich, And he who waters will also be watered himself.*

Ecclesiastes 11:4 (NLT)

4 *If you wait for perfect conditions, you will never get anything done.*

Galatians 6:7 (NKJV)

7 *Do not be deceived, God is not mocked; for whatever a man sows, that he will also reap.*

2 Corinthians 9:6-7 (NLT)

6 *Remember this—a farmer who plants only a few seeds will get a small crop. But the one who plants generously will get a generous crop.* 7 *You must each make up your own mind as to how much you should give. Don't give reluctantly or in response to pressure. For God loves the person who gives cheerfully.*

Giving (above and beyond the tithe)

Remember the financial priorities laid out for us in scripture. Any surplus we have is to go towards debt first, savings/ investing or giving second.

CORRECT FINANCIAL PRIORITIES

- Finances:
  a. God – Tithe
  b. Taxes
  c. Needs
  d. Surplus
     1. Debt
     2. Savings & Investing & Giving

Giving to other Christians

Galatians 6:10 (NLT)

[10]Whenever we have the opportunity, we should do good to everyone, especially to our Christian brothers and sisters.

1 John 3:17 (NLT)

[17]But if anyone has enough money to live well, and sees a brother or sister in need and refuses to help—how can God's love be in that person?

James 2:15-16 (NLT)

[15]Suppose you see a brother or sister who needs food or clothing,
[16]and you say, "Well, good-bye and God bless you; stay warm and eat well"—but then you don't give that person any food or clothing. What good does that do?

2 Corinthians 8:14 (NLT)

[14]Right now you have plenty and can help them. Then at some other time they can share with you when you need it. In this way, everyone's needs will be met.

Romans 12:13 (NLT)

[13]When God's children are in need, be the one to help them out. And get into the habit of inviting guests home for dinner or, if they need lodging, for the night.

Acts 11:29 (NLT)

[29]So the believers in Antioch decided to send relief to the brothers and sisters in Judea, everyone giving as much as they could.

Giving to the poor

1 Corinthians 16:1-2 (NLT)

[1]Now about the money being collected for the Christians in Jerusalem: You should follow the same procedures I gave to the churches in Galatia. [2]On every Lord's Day, each of you should put aside some amount of money in relation to what you have earned and save it for this offering. Don't wait until I get there and then try to collect it all at once.

Why do you think God wants us to help the poor?

____

____

____

____

____

____

____

____

Proverbs 14:21 (NASB)

[21]He who despises his neighbor sins, But happy is he who is gracious to the poor.

Proverbs 14:31 (NASB)

[31]He who oppresses the poor taunts his Maker, But he who is gracious to the needy honors Him.

Proverbs 19:17 (NASB)

[17]One who is gracious to a poor man lends to the LORD, And He will repay him for his good deed.

Proverbs 21:13 (NASB)

13He who shuts his ear to the cry of the poor Will also cry himself and not be answered.

Proverbs 22:9 (NASB)

9He who is generous will be blessed, For he gives some of his food to the poor.

Proverbs 28:27 (NASB)

27He who gives to the poor will never want, But he who shuts his eyes will have many curses.

Luke 3:11 (NLT)

11John replied, "If you have two coats, give one to the poor. If you have food, share it with those who are hungry."

Isaiah 58:10 (TLB)—see also NASB

10Feed the hungry! Help those in trouble! Then your light will shine out from the darkness, and the darkness around you shall be as bright as day.

Ezekiel 16:49 (NLT)

49Sodom's sins were pride, laziness, and gluttony, while the poor and needy suffered outside her door.

Here is an interesting fact:
Only 15-20% of all Christians tithe.
Can you imagine if all of them tithed?
There would be no need for welfare or poverty. There would be more than enough for everyone with much left over besides.

Giving to your family and relatives

Mark 7:10-12 (NLT)

10For instance, Moses gave you this law from God: "Honor your father and mother," and "Anyone who speaks evil of father or mother must be put to death." 11But you say it is all right for people to say to their parents, "Sorry, I can't help you. For I have vowed to give to God what I could have given to you. 12You let them disregard their needy parents."

1 Timothy 5:8 (NKJV)

8But if anyone does not provide for his own, and especially for those of his household, he has denied the faith and is worse than an unbeliever.

1 Timothy 5:3-4, 16 (NLT)

3The church should care for any widow who has no one else to care for her. 4But if she has children or grandchildren, their first responsibility is to show godliness at home and repay their parents by taking care of them. This is something that pleases God very much.

16If a Christian woman has relatives who are widows, she must take care of them and not put the responsibility on the church. Then the church can care for widows who are truly alone.

Mark 4:24 (NASB)

24And He was saying to them, "Take care what you listen to. By your standard of measure it will be measured to you; and more will be given you besides."

2 Corinthians 9:6 (NLT)

6Remember this—a farmer who plants only a few seeds will get a small crop. But the one who plants generously will get a generous crop.

What are "alms"? (giving in secret to the poor)

Definition of "alms"—Anything given gratuitously to relieve the poor, as money, food, or clothing; a gift of charity.

Chapter synthesis

In this chapter we examined scriptures that tell us about tithing and giving. We saw that churches need to tithe too. The church needs to set the example for its members. The fact is that if every believer and every church tithed, there would be no poverty and no need for welfare.

Notes and reflections…

Chapter 10: Saving and Investing

In This Chapter

- Saving
- The three types of savings
- Investing
- Godly reasons to invest and accumulate wealth
- How to create wealth

When we follow our commitments to live within our means, and not to borrow again, no matter what circumstances arise, it will be desirous for us to establish a savings program.

We need to save for expenses which come up seasonally, annually and periodically. For example, the insurance on your house may come due annually. It would be wise to save one twelfth each month so that when the payment comes due you have the money to pay the premium. Some expenses, such as vacation and auto repairs, do not come due every month. We need to estimate how much we spend for these on a yearly basis, then save one-twelfth each month in advance.

Sometimes our income is seasonal, or sporadic, like that of a commissioned salesman. We should make a conservative estimate as to how much we need per month to meet our financial objectives. Then we make a commitment to save up for the months ahead when the income will be low.

The problem is that *we have been taught to spend.* Saving for seasonal needs is difficult at first, but with God all things are possible.

In most places where we live today, we need an automobile for transportation. God's Word tells us that we should not borrow, which by necessity then requires of us to save so that we can buy large items such as automobiles, furniture, and the like, without borrowing. Saving for future replacements requires self-discipline, dedication and commitment.

The Bible tells us that it is wise for us to save for the future. We cannot take anything with us. If we leave a good foundation in God's Word for our children, this will be a better inheritance than money.

Saving for future replacements requires self-discipline, dedication, and commitment.

When we accumulate savings, we need to be cautious that *we do not take pride in what we have and trust in our money rather than in God.* We need to remember that we are stewards of that which belongs to Him. To those who are faithful with little, more will be given. But if we fix our hope on the money and possessions of this world, they will be taken away. Our future is not in our savings but in God who richly supplies all our needs. Our savings require from us stewardship—responsibility, accountability, and faithfulness.

As stewards of God's money, we need to be careful to evaluate each situation and investment opportunity to assure that whatever we do is in agreement with God's Word. When we do this we will find that there are, in reality, not that many investments which pass this test. For example, God's Word tells us not to borrow, and this eliminates a large portion of potential investments.

We need to remember that as stewards we have no choice but to follow the direction and guidance of God. When we turn to Him for answers, He always gives them. By His wisdom a house or household is built, and by our understanding of Him it will be established.

There are investments which are scriptural. For example, as long as we still have debt, our best investment is our debt. The scriptures tell us that we are not to withhold payment from our creditors when we have the means to pay them back. If we have a business, our investment might be in the growth and expansion of it. Other investments are various savings programs such as annuities, U.S. Treasury Bills and bonds, savings programs, or even stocks and bonds. It is good to diversify, as the scriptures tell us.

Saving

We have been taught to *spend*, we have not been taught to *save*.

The Bible tells us it is good to save for the future. It also warns us not to put our trust in our money, but to put our trust in God.

A penny saved is more than a penny earned

The penny earned is subject to various taxes. If you save $100 by choosing some alternative product, it would be equivalent to earning $140 to $150 ($140 less taxes may be net $100).

One way to start a savings plan, even if you believe you have no money left over to save, is to put a glass jar in the middle of your kitchen table. The jar should be glass so everyone can see the progress. A single individual, or a family, is then challenged to save $1 per day and put it in the jar. It should not be your intention to use $1 from your billfold to deposit into the jar on a daily basis. It should be the challenge of each household member to pay attention to their individual spending or buying habits. For example, if you stop every morning at a convenience store to buy a cup of coffee for $1.50, you could decide to have a smaller cup for 75 cents, or you could decide to have a cup at home. Another example: if you are about to buy a certain sandwich for lunch, instead you make a conscious decision to choose an alternative sandwich that costs less.

The key here is to pay attention to your habits, make a conscious effort to choose an alternative and identify the resulting savings. These savings then are deposited into the glass jar. Your goal is to save at least $1 per day.

When you try this savings challenge, you will be amazed by how much control you have over how much you are willing to spend. The savings will quickly multiply. The resulting savings are actually money you saved that would be gone, or spent, had you not made a decision to choose an alternative. Based on the fact that these savings represent "would have been spent" money, you could put them away as long-term savings and forget about them. Or you could use these funds to reduce your debt.

The average household can save $150 to $250 per month by making smart choices.

The scriptures encourage us to save

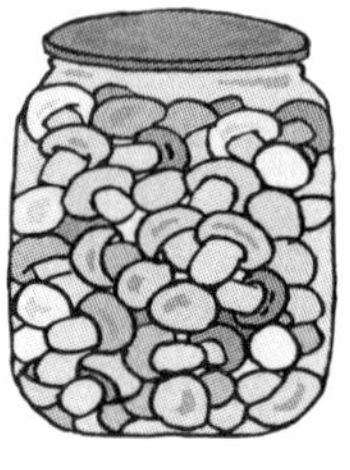

Proverbs 21:20 (TLB)—see also NIV

[20]The wise man saves for the future, but the foolish man spends whatever he gets.

Proverbs 22:3 (TLB)—see also NIV

[3]A prudent man foresees the difficulties ahead and prepares for them; the simpleton goes blindly on and suffers the consequences.

Matthew 6:19-21 (NASB)

[19]Do not store up for yourselves treasures on earth, where moth and rust destroy, and where thieves break in and steal. [20]But store up for yourselves treasures in heaven, where neither moth nor rust destroys, and where thieves do not break in or steal; [21]for where your treasure is, there your heart will be also.

Proverbs 11:28 (TLB)—see also NASB

28 Trust in your money and down you go! Trust in God and flourish as a tree!

Proverbs 10:5 (NASB)

5 He who gathers in summer is a son who acts wisely, But he who sleeps in harvest is a son who acts shamefully.

Is it easier for you to trust your money or God? Why?

____

____

____

____

____

____

____

____

Luke 12:15 (NASB)

15 Then He said to them, "Beware, and be on your guard against every form of greed; for not even when one has an abundance does his life consist of his possessions."

There are three types of savings

1. Budgetary savings
2. Emergency and replacement savings
3. Long-term savings/investments

Budgetary savings

Budgetary savings is an amount saved each month to cover planned and unplanned expenses that are not incurred equally each month. This type of saving is essential for an effective, functioning budget. For example, if car insurance premiums of $420 come due every six months, $70 per month needs to be saved. Failure to provide for budgetary savings is a budget buster and leads to borrowing. Savings for unexpected repairs fall into this category.

Budgetary savings are also used to even out seasonal expenditures such as clothing.

Annual clothing costs should be saved on a monthly basis until needed.

Budgetary savings also are used to even out large swings in income during the year. A school teacher may elect to be paid over nine months instead of having the salary paid out over twelve months. Each month a portion of the salary must be saved to carry the teacher through the three months when no salary is paid.

Construction workers and many self-employed individuals often find their income is uneven and/or seasonal. They must utilize budgetary savings to even out the flow of money.

Budgetary savings should be segregated into a savings account that permits ready access to the funds. Why are budgetary savings important for you?

____

____

____

____

____

____

____

Emergency and replacement savings

After satisfying the need for budgetary savings, one should begin to accumulate savings for emergencies and to replace large items that wear out or break down and can no longer be repaired. Examples of those items are automobile, appliances, and furniture.

There are a wide variety of emergencies that may overtake you and destroy your budget. In this present day, it is increasingly likely that an individual will experience different periods of unemployment. This is an emergency that one can and should prepare for. Each family, or household, should have sufficient savings to replace the take-home pay of its highest wage earner for a period of at least six months.

Emergency and replacement savings should be in separate accounts with 90-day or six-month notice, permitting ready access as needed. Why is it important to save now for future replacements?

____

____

____

Long-term savings/investments

The third type of savings is for long-term purposes. Saving for the children's college education and saving for retirement are vital. The best investment strategy is to adopt a plan of steady continual contributions to accounts allowing time and compounding to build your savings.

Investing

The scriptures have much to say about investing.

Ecclesiastes 5:13-15 (NASB)

13-14There is a grievous evil which I have seen under the sun: riches being hoarded by their owner to his hurt. When those riches were lost through a bad investment and he had fathered a son, then there was nothing to support him. 15As he had come naked from his mother's womb, so will he return as he came. He will take nothing from the fruit of his labor that he can carry in his hand.

1 Timothy 6:17 (NASB)

17Instruct those who are rich in this present world not to be conceited or to fix their hope on the uncertainty of riches, but on God, who richly supplies us with all things to enjoy.

Proverbs 28:20 (NLT)

20The trustworthy will get a rich reward. But the person who wants to get rich quick will only get into trouble.

Proverbs 28:22 (TLB)—see also NIV

22Trying to get rich quick is evil and leads to poverty.

Proverbs 15:16 (NLT)

[16]*It is better to have little with fear for the LORD than to have great treasure with turmoil.*

1 Timothy 6:6-7 (TLB)—see also NASB

[6]*Do you want to be truly rich? You already are if you are happy and good.* [7]*After all, we didn't bring any money with us when we came into the world, and we can't carry away a single penny when we die.*

Luke 12:16-21 (NASB)

[16]*And He told them a parable, saying, "The land of a rich man was very productive.* [17]*And he began reasoning to himself, saying, 'What shall I do, since I have no place to store my crops?'*
[18]*Then he said, 'This is what I will do: I will tear down my barns and build larger ones, and there I will store all my grain and my goods.* [19]*'And I will say to my soul, "Soul, you have many goods laid up for many years to come; take your ease, eat, drink and be merry."'* [20]*But God said to him, 'You fool! This very night your soul is required of you; and now who will own what you have prepared?'* [21]*So is the man who stores up treasure for himself, and is not rich toward God."*

Proverbs 21:5 (NLT)

[5]*Good planning and hard work lead to prosperity, but hasty shortcuts lead to poverty.*

2 Corinthians 6:14 (NKJV)

[14]*Do not be unequally yoked together with unbelievers. For what fellowship has righteousness with lawlessness? And what communion has light with darkness?*

Don't consider investing until the following steps have taken place

1. You are tithing faithfully and consistently
2. Your consumer debts are paid off—Remember, your best investment is your debt
3. A rapid reduction program is in place for long-term debt

4. A budgetary savings account is in place
5. Emergency and replacement savings have been established

Ecclesiastes 3:1 (NASB)

1There is an appointed time for everything. And there is a time for every event under heaven.

Ecclesiastes 8:6 (NLT)

6Yes, there is a time and a way for everything, even as people's troubles lie heavily upon them.

God approves of investing

Luke 19:12-26 (NLT)

12He said, "A nobleman was called away to a distant empire
to be crowned king and then return. 13Before he left, he called
together ten servants and gave them ten pounds of silver to
invest for him while he was gone. 14But his people hated him
and sent a delegation after him to say they did not want him to be their king.

15When he returned, the king called in the servants to whom he had given the money. He wanted to find out what they had done
with the money and what their profits were. 16The first servant
reported a tremendous gain—ten times as much as the original
amount! 17'Well done!' the king exclaimed. 'You are a trustworthy servant. You have been faithful with the little I entrusted to you, so you will be governor of ten cities as your reward.'

18The next servant also reported a good gain—five times the
original amount. 19'Well done!' the king said. 'You can be governor over five cities.'

20But the third servant brought back only the original amount of
money and said, 'I hid it and kept it safe. 21I was afraid because
you are a hard man to deal with, taking what isn't yours and harvesting crops you didn't plant.'

22'You wicked servant!' the king roared. 'Hard, am I? If you knew
so much about me and how tough I am, 23why didn't you deposit

the money in the bank so I could at least get some interest on it?'
24Then turning to the others standing nearby, the king ordered, 'Take the money from this servant, and give it to the one who earned the most.'

25'But, master,' they said, 'that servant has enough already!'

26'Yes,' the king replied, 'but to those who use well what they are given, even more will be given. But from those who are unfaithful, even what little they have will be taken away.'"

Matthew 25:14-30 gives another perspective on this story:

- Everything we have comes from God
- Doing things God's way is usually the opposite of man's way
- Wise money management pleases God
- Poor money management displeases God

Godly reasons to invest and accumulate wealth

To leave an inheritance

Proverbs 13:22 (TLB)—see also NKJV

22When a good man dies, he leaves an inheritance to his grandchildren; but when a sinner dies, his wealth is stored up for the godly.

2 Corinthians 12:14 (NASB)

14Here for this third time I am ready to come to you, and I will not be a burden to you; for I do not seek what is yours, but you; for children are not responsible to save up for their parents, but parents for their children.

To provide for college and other assistance to your household

1 Timothy 5:8 (NASB)

[8]But if anyone does not provide for his own, and especially for those of his household, he has denied the faith and is worse than an unbeliever.

How to create wealth

It is essential that Christians not get caught up in the lure of riches when investing to build wealth. The rate of return that one might earn is always a function of risk. The greater the potential gain, the greater the potential risk of loss.

Psalm 62:10 (NKJV)

[10]Do not trust in oppression, nor vainly hope in robbery; If riches increase, do not set your heart on them.

Proverbs 28:20 (TLB)—see also NKJV

[20]The man who wants to do right will get a rich reward. But the man who wants to get rich quick will quickly fail.

Four things are required to build much wealth

1. Time
2. Self-discipline
3. Knowledge
4. Planning

1. Time – the magic of compounding

The best investment strategy is to save even a small amount of money, systematically over a long period of time. Through the magic of compounding, the amount accumulated will be far beyond most people's expectations.

Proverbs 13:11 (NLT)

[11]*Wealth from get-rich-quick schemes quickly disappears; wealth from hard work grows.*

The power of $100 per month ($3.23 per day)

Years	Total Invested	5% Return	10% Return	15% Return	20% Return
10	$12,000	$15,528	$20,485	$27,522	$37,610
15	18,000	26,729	41,447	66,651	111,570
20	24,000	41,103	75,937	149,724	310,965
25	30,000	59,551	132,683	324,353	848,529
30	36,000	83,226	226,049	692,328	2,297784
35	42,000	113,609	379,664	1,457,718	6,204,932
40	48,000	152,602	632,408	3,101,605	16,738,488
45	54,000	202,644	1,048,250	6,544,503	45,136,640
50	60,000	266,865	1,732,439	13,799,311	121,697,208
55	66,000	349,284	2,858,141	29,086,509	328,102,216
60	72,000	455,058	4,710,269	61,299,407	884,563,952
65	78,000	590,803	7,757,591	129,177,824	2,384,768,178
70	84,000	765,013	12,771,378	272,209,958	6,429,273,974

Begin as early in life as possible

If a young person saves $100 per month, or $1,200 per year, in a tax-free account (IRA) between the ages of 20 and 26 (for seven years) he or she will have contributed a total of $8,400. Then if he or she never contributes another dime over the next 38 years, an account yielding 15% annually will at age 65 accumulate to $2,689,808.

But notice the consequences of waiting

If he or she had waited until age 27 to make the first contribution and after that contributed $1,200 systematically for the next 38 years, he or she will have contributed $45,600 by age 65. The same type of account yielding 15% will accumulate to $1,612,347. The difference is over $1,000,000.

THE TIME TO START IS NOW!!!

Remember earlier we spoke of saving $1.00 per day in a glass jar? See what happens if you put away $30 per month for a long period of time.

The power of $1.00 per day

Years	Total Invested	5% Return	10% Return	15% Return	20% Return
10	$3,600	$4,658	$6,145	$8,257	**$11,283**
20	7,200	12,331	22,781	44,917	**93,290**
30	10,800	24,968	67,815	207,698	**689,335**
40	14,400	45,781	189,722	930,482	**5,021,546**
50	18,000	80,060	519,732	4,139,793	**36,509,163**

2. Self Discipline

You must have or develop self-discipline. Pretend the savings and investments are "spent" or into long-term arrangements that cannot be touched until your long-term goals are reached. You cannot eat your seed. Reject the lifestyle which would have you consume all you have.

Remember we are stewards of that which God entrusted to us. He who is faithful with a little, to him shall more be given.

1 Corinthians 4:7(b) (NLT)

And if all you have is from God, why boast as though you have accomplished something on your own?

1 Corinthians 4:2 (NLT)

2*Now, a person who is put in charge as a manager must be faithful.*

3. Knowledge

We have been told that we perish for lack of knowledge. It is important to invest time and effort in knowledge.

Proverbs 23:23 (NLT)

23*Get the truth and don't ever sell it; also get wisdom, discipline, and discernment.*

Read magazines and books that help you to understand when and in what to invest. Take career advancing seminars and listen to audio tapes or video tapes. In other words, invest in knowledge. *Knowledge* minimizes risk.

Know when and where to invest and where not to invest:

- Invest in your debt—your best investment is your debt!
- Invest in your own business

Proverbs 16:11 (TLB)—see also NASB

[11]The Lord demands fairness in every business deal. He established this principle.

The Bible warns about partnerships

2 Corinthians 6:14-17 (NLT)

[14]Don't team up with those who are unbelievers. How can goodness be a partner with wickedness? How can light live with darkness? [15]What harmony can there be between Christ and the Devil? How can a believer be a partner with an unbeliever? [16]And what union can there be between God's temple and idols? For we are the temple of the living God. As God said:

"I will live in them and walk among them. I will be their God, and they will be My people. [17]Therefore, come out from them and separate yourselves from them," says the Lord. "Don't touch their filthy things, and I will welcome you."

Have you teamed up with anyone you shouldn't have?

What did you learn?

___

___

___

___

___

___

___

___

Avoid risky investments

Remember the rate of return is proportionate with the risk of loss.

Ecclesiastes 5:13-14, (NASB)

13-14 There is a grievous evil which I have seen under the sun: riches being hoarded by their owner to his hurt. When those riches were lost through a bad investment and he had fathered a son, then there was nothing to support him.

The Bible tells us to diversify our investments

Ecclesiastes 11:2 (NASB)

2 Divide your portion to seven, or even to eight, for you do not know what misfortune may occur on the earth.

- **Real estate**—home, investment properties, reits, mutual funds
- **Equity security**—your own business, stocks, mutual funds
- **Debt securities**—loans to others, bonds, mutual funds

- **Government securities**—T-bills, notes, E-bonds, I-bonds, mutual funds
- **Insurance contracts** —annuities
- **Hard assets**—gold, silver, other metals, oil
- **Collectible art**—paintings, sculptures, other collectibles
- **Bank**—CDs, MM accounts, savings accounts

4. Planning

The Bible tells us that it is important to have a plan. The subject of planning is discussed in Chapter 11.

Which of these four requirements for wealth do you struggle with? Why do you think that is?

Chapter synthesis

As we saw in this chapter, scriptures tell us that it is good to save for the future. But the Bible warns us not to put our trust in our investments, but in God. It further warns us about all sorts of investments and get-rich-quick schemes. A plan of steady savings seems to be the best answer.

Notes and reflections…

Chapter 11: Planning for Success

In This Chapter

- Why do we need a plan?
- Setting goals
- Suggested financial goals
- What is a spending plan?
- Spending priorities

God has a plan for us. In Romans, Paul tells us that God knew us even before we were born. He predestined us to become conformed to the image of His Son, Jesus. We were called to be justified, and also to be glorified.

Since God has a plan for us, we need to determine what that plan is so that our plans coincide with His Plan for us. Otherwise our plans will be in vain. God tells us that there is a plan deep in our heart (spirit) but only when understand God's will (attain wisdom) can we draw out that plan and understand it. This plan which God has for us is sometimes referred to as our blueprint.

It is obvious that we need a plan. Without a plan we can get in all sorts of trouble, and then we scramble and *try to make things work.* It usually ends up the world's way instead of God's way. Rather than letting this situation arise, we need to plan. If our plan is in line with God's plan, we will not run out of money or resources after we lay the foundation. God's plan is complete and lacking in nothing. The Lord tells us that we should plan. We need to commit our plans to Him so He can establish our steps accordingly.

We have to be cautious to make sure we are within God's plan for our life. Without a plan we are like a ship without a rudder and in the middle of the sea, hopelessly drifting. The same is true for any enterprise, whether a household of a single person, a family unit, a business or even a church. God's Word states, planning (wisdom), becomes strong through common sense (understanding), and profits wonderfully by keeping abreast of the facts (knowledge).

An enterprise, whether it's the household of a single person or that of a family, business or church, should develop a long-range plan according to its respective purpose. This plan of broad objectives should express the mission, vision, and ethical tone of the enterprise. As discussed in earlier chapters, it is vitally important for us to recognize that we need to put God—and knowing His will—as our number one objective. Once a long-range plan has been established, *we need to set goals.*

Goals are the end result toward which we intend to direct our effort. Interim goals, or sub-goals, are intermediary steps which are realistic and can be achieved. They eventually lead to the ultimately expected goals. For example, if we set for ourselves a goal to read through the entire Bible in thirty days, we probably could do it, however, at the expense of other basic individual and family needs. A more realistic goal would be to study the New Testament in one year. Attainable goals may be to read five chapters per week, which would lead to the desired end result (there are 260 chapters in the New Testament). Goals should be realistic, meaningful, attainable, and fun. Goals which are unrealistic are futile and lead to discouragement. They should be flexible and need to be evaluated and readjusted periodically. Remember, Rome was not built in one day. Neither will we reach all our expected goals in one day.

Goals without the intention of doing anything to bring about the desired results are meaningless. *We have to make a commitment to take action.* It is difficult for us to give up our "safety zones" or complacency. In the Webster's New Collegiate Dictionary complacency is defined as "self-satisfaction accompanied by unawareness of actual dangers or deficiencies." God's Word tells us that we are not to pursue selfish ambitions but that we are to do according to His Word.

God's Word tells us that *we need to act on His Word.* That means we need to do just what it says. His Word is our foundation which cannot be shaken. Our complacency is a deception whereby Satan can keep in control of us, and thereby keep us from realizing the full blessings which God has promised to us.

Jesus is not talking about the unbeliever. He is talking about we who have heard His Word, but refuse to believe enough to act and stand on it. When we are ready to take action on the Word of God, it is helpful to make a commitment to Him to that effect. When we make that commitment to Him, He will see us through.

In this chapter we will look at some suggested financial goals.

Living within our means

Our first thought, when thinking of living within our means, probably causes us to become defensive. We tend to justify every financial decision and think of reasons why the spending was necessary or a good investment. There is social pressure to own more "things." Then we buy so many "things" that we need more "things" to haul them around in, or to store them in. We have been taught to spend, whether we have the resources or not. Our attitudes have been programmed to believe that we need "things" regardless of cost. The use of credit has been made available to buy instantly. These are obstacles, and when acted upon, this is where financial bondage occurs.

I have seen many families not living within their means. It does not matter how much or how little money they have, it just is not enough. This is true whether it be the single person, who seemingly could not make it on $500 per month, to the family man who could not make it on $9,000 per month. The symptoms were the same in both instances. Both were overspending.

Only the causes, which were discussed in Chapter 3, were slightly different. Often it is a painful process to look at oneself to identify the causes. *It takes God's help, hard effort, and persistence to change our attitudes and habits.*

As in all matters concerning our lives, we need to turn to the Word of God and see what He says about what we should do. First we need to recall that we are stewards of that which God has entrusted to us. *The three key elements of stewardship are Responsibility, Accountability, and Faithfulness.* To become good stewards we cannot permit ourselves to be led by the ways of the world, which we were taught. Instead, we must turn to God's ways and trust Him. Our trust is not to be in things of the world but in God Himself. His Word tells us that we should be content and live within our means.

God wants us to prosper. That is what He has promised in His Word. However, as long as we are led by the things of the world, which includes the love of money, why would He give us the very thing which would only destroy us? When we learn to be content, no matter what our circumstances are, and permit Him to lead us along the path which He has chosen for us, then we will live in prosperity. When we are faithful with a few things (like putting His Word into action) then He will put us in charge of many things.

Our trust is not to be in the things of the world but in God Himself

To be obedient to God's Word, and live within our means, we have to make an effort not to spend more than what we have. When we make a commitment to start living within our means, we need to evaluate every purchase or expenditure prior to spending.

We have to determine whether what we intend to buy is a need, a want, or a desire. This takes the cooperation of every member of the family. In the beginning there will be disagreements as to whether the expenditure is a need, a want or a desire. Take courage, turn to the Lord, Who will guide and direct you. Patience is a virtue which God intends for us to learn.

The Word talks about needs, wants and desires. Needs are food, shelter and clothing. Wants involve choices about quality. If we are faithful, He gives us the desires of our heart.

As long as we are not living within our means we will remain in financial bondage. To become free, we have to take action. Make a commitment to live within your means. Make a plan to live within your means and ask God to help you. Ask God to let you know what His plan is for you. *It takes God's help, hard effort, and persistence to change our attitudes and habits. To be obedient to God's Word, and live within our means, we have to make an effort not to spend more than what we have.*

In this chapter we will discuss ways to deal with an out-of-balance spending plan (budget). A spending plan is a plan designed as a guideline to operate an enterprise (household, business or church) within limitations. Expected expenditures are limited to expected income. To make a spending plan work requires discipline and certain commitments to assure that the expenditures do not exceed the income. We need to determine precisely how much money is earned and how much is spent each month. If we are borrowing from the bank, or are adding to charge cards, we most likely are spending more than our earnings. Our total current expenditures, which include operating expenses, debt payments, as well as purchases on credit (new charges or loans), should not exceed our total current earnings. If they do, we have an out-of- balance budget.

Since we have determined that we are stewards of God's property, we are accountable to Him for our actions. The first thing to do when we realize that our budget is out of balance is to face up to it and not to hide it. God knows our hearts and our motives and He also forgives.

Earlier we discussed the need to make a commitment to live within our means. If we want to be free from the bondage of finance, *we have to make the decision to do something about the problem. We have to discipline our thinking and our spending habits.* Satan would want us to believe that there is no way, or why bother, or it will not work anyway. Remember, he is a liar and it is his intent to keep us in financial bondage. Instead, we must resist Satan and stand on the Word of God.

When we ask God to forgive us for having made a mess of our finances, He always forgives. We should confess our mistakes, repent and ask forgiveness. To repent means to turn from sin and dedicate ourselves to changing our lives to what God intended them to be. We must turn over our assets and liabilities to God, confess that they are His, and seek His help to get our finances back in order. Turning things over involves the confession that we are mere stewards of that which He entrusted to us, and that we will seek guidance form His Word as to how we should manage as His servants.

When Christ gave His life for us, He did so to set us free. It is relatively easy for us to accept that we have been saved. When we ask ourselves, "Saved from what?" we realize that we were saved from all evil, unprofitable things when He went to the cross. We were saved from sickness and disease and from every form of bondage—which includes the bondage of finances. Satan tells us that we have to get our bills caught up first before we can be free. He knows that we have been following his ways when it comes to finances and that we are being consumed by greed and want so that we will never get caught up. We have to resist the devil and turn our problems over to God. He will show us that we have already been set free by Jesus Christ. The battle was over more than two thousand years ago and victory over financial bondage is ours; this is evidenced by the scriptures. We are not to turn our backs on the problems or obligations and think that they will go away. We know in our hearts that God will show us how to deal with the problems and how to solve them. We are to refuse to focus on the problem, or be consumed by the apparent lack of progress. Instead we must focus on God and trust Him for the answer. God is on our side. We cannot lose.

Why do we need a plan?

Did you know that God has a plan for each and every one of us? We need to pray and seek God's plan for us so our plan coincides with His plan for us.

Ephesians 1:16(b)-18 (NLT)

I pray for you constantly, 17asking God, the glorious Father of our Lord Jesus Christ, to give you spiritual wisdom and understanding, so that you might grow in your knowledge of God. [18]I pray that your hearts will be flooded with light so that you can understand the wonderful future He has promised to those He called. I want you to realize what a rich and glorious inheritance he has given to His people.

A long time ago, a young pastor told me that to find God's plan for my life, I needed to pray Ephesians 1:18 every day, as often as possible each day, for thirty days. At the end of that time, I would know God's plan for my life. He was right. Here is Ephesians 1:18 paraphrased:

I pray that the Lord would open the eyes of my heart that I may know the true purpose of His calling on my life.

Romans 8:28-30 (NASB)

[28]And we know that God causes all things to work together for good to those who love God, to those who are called according to His purpose. [29]For those whom He foreknew, He also predestined to become conformed to the image of His Son, so that He would be the firstborn among many brethren; [30]and these whom He predestined, He also called; and these whom He called, He also justified; and these whom He justified, He also glorified.

There is a plan (blueprint) for our life deep within our heart but we must have understanding to draw it out.

What is God's plan for your life?

____

____

____

____

____

____

____

Proverbs 20:5 (NASB)

[5]A plan in the heart of a man is like deep water, but a man of understanding draws it out.

Proverbs 2:3-6 (NLT)

[3]Cry out for insight and understanding. [4]Search for them as you would for lost money or hidden treasure. [5]Then you will understand what it means to fear the LORD, and you will gain knowledge of God. [6]For the LORD grants wisdom! From His mouth come knowledge and understanding.

Why should you cry out for insight and understanding?

____

____

____

____

____

____

____

____

God has a plan for you, your blueprint

Jeremiah 29:11 (NASB)

[11]"For I know the plans that I have for you," declares the LORD, "plans for welfare and not for calamity to give you a future and a hope."

Without a plan we get into all sorts of problems, then scramble to try to make things work, usually choosing the world's way instead of God's way. Without a plan we are like a ship without a rudder, drifting aimlessly. This applies to any enterprise, whether a household, family, business, or any other enterprise.

You need to plan!

Luke 14:28-30 (NASB)

28"For which one of you, when he wants to build a tower, does not first sit down and calculate the cost to see if he has enough to complete it? 29"Otherwise, when he has laid a foundation and is not able to finish, all who observe it begin to ridicule him, 30saying, 'This man began to build and was not able to finish.'

The Lord tells us to plan and commit our plans to Him

Proverbs 16:3 (NLT)

3Commit your work to the LORD, and then your plans will succeed.

How can you commit your plans to the Lord?

____

____

____

____

____

____

____

____

Proverbs 16:9 (NASB)

9The mind of man plans his way, But the LORD directs his steps.

Psalm 37:23 (NASB)

23The steps of a man are established by the LORD, And He delights in his way.

Proverbs 24:3-4 (TLB)—author's explanation (see also NASB)

Any enterprise (a home or other entity) built by wise planning (wisdom), becomes strong through common sense (understanding) and profits wonderfully by keeping abreast of the facts (knowledge).

Setting goals

To achieve your goals for the years ahead, you must plan your course of action now. You know that what you do today will have an effect on what your family will be like five years from now. Without goals we tend to be task-oriented rather than results-oriented. *Goals are the results and rewards of our efforts.*

Be aware of your expectations when setting goals

Remember, a step taken too fast may cause discouragement. Often, the desired long-range goals are difficult to achieve and require hard work and effort. Take one step at a time and allow yourself time to experience the joy of having reached that goal.

If you find that the goals you started with are not realistic, or if you need to take more time, change your goals. You must be flexible and allow for changes.

What is your long-range plan?
What interim goal do you have?

___

___

___

___

___

___

___

Take the time to celebrate small victories

Goals are the end result toward which we intend to direct our efforts, but setting goals without taking action is worthless.

Take action! Be a doer!

Romans 2:13 (NASB)

[13]...for it is not the hearers of the Law who are just before God, but the doers of the Law will be justified.

James 1:22-25 (NASB)

*[22]But prove yourselves doers of the Word, and not merely hearers
who delude themselves. [23]For if anyone is a hearer of the Word
and not a doer, he is like a man who looks at his natural face
in a mirror; [24]for once he has looked at himself and gone away,
he has immediately forgotten what kind of person he was. [25]But
one who looks intently at the perfect law, the law of liberty,
and abides by it, not having become a forgetful hearer but an
effectual doer, this man will be blessed in what he does.*

Ephesians 6:6-9 (NLT)

*[6]Work hard, but not just to please your masters when they are
watching. As slaves of Christ, do the will of god with all your
heart. [7]Work with enthusiasm, as though you were working for
the Lord rather than for people. [8]Remember that the Lord will
reward each one of us for the good we do, whether we are slaves
or free. [9]And in the same way, you masters must treat your
slaves right. Don't threaten them; remember, you both have the
same Master in heaven and he has no favorites.*

Matthew 7:21 (NASB)—see context

[21]Not everyone who says to Me, "Lord, Lord," will enter the kingdom of heaven, but he who does the will of My Father who is in heaven will enter.

Luke 6:46-49 (NLT)

*[46]So why do you call me "Lord," when you won't obey me? [47]I
will show you what it's like when someone comes to Me, listens
to My teaching, and then obeys Me. [48]It is like a person who
builds a house on a strong foundation laid upon the underlying*

rock. When the floodwaters rise and break against the house, it stands firm because it is well built. [49]*But anyone who listens and doesn't obey is like a person who builds a house without a foundation. When the floods sweep down against that house, it will crumble into a heap of ruins.*

Setting goals for a long-range family or household plan

What is a "long-range" plan? We have been taught to expect instant solutions to everything. We watch a TV program in thirty minutes, the plot develops and the story concludes all in thirty minutes. We have the same expectations for everything else in life. Instead, your plan should cover months and even years. Remember, it took years to get your family situation or finances into the state they are, it will take some time to get the problems or issues resolved.

Ask God to help you stay *focused.* 1 Peter 1:13 (NASB) "Therefore, prepare your minds for action (discipline your thinking), keep sober in spirit, fix your hope completely on the grace to be brought to you at the revelation of Jesus Christ."

Pray together as a family about:

- The house you live in
- The car you drive
- Where you should work
- Whether both spouses need to work

A family that prays together stays together!

Suggested financial goals

- Living within your means
- Becoming debt free (Chapters 7 & 8)
- Regular tithing and giving (Chapter 9)
- Regular saving and investing (Chapter 10)

What obstacles keep your family from praying together?

____

____

____

____

____

____

____

Living within your means

Luke 3:14 (NASB)

[14]Some soldiers were questioning Him, saying, "And what about us, what shall we do?" And He said to them, "Do not take money from anyone by force, or accuse anyone falsely, and be content with your wages."

Philippians 4:11-13 (NASB)

[11]Not that I speak from want, for I have learned to be content
in whatever circumstances I am. [12]I know how to get along with
humble means, and I also know how to live in prosperity; in any and every circumstance I have learned the secret of being filled and going hungry, both of having abundance and suffering
need. [13]I can do all things through Him who strengthens me.

Establish Priorities by discussing the differences between *needs*, *wants*, and *desires*.

Needs

- Food, shelter, clothing

1Timothy 6:8 (NLT)—see context

[8]So if we have enough food and clothing, let us be content.

Wants

- ❋ More than a need, it involves choices and quality

1 Peter 3:3-4 (NASB)

[3]Your adornment must not be merely external—braiding the hair, and wearing gold jewelry, or putting on dresses; [4]but let it be the hidden person of the heart, with the imperishable quality of a gentle and quiet spirit, which is precious in the sight of God.

Desires

- ❋ Longing for worldly objects

1 John 2:15-16 (NASB)

[15]Do not love the world nor the things in the world. If anyone loves the world, the love of the Father is not in him. [16]For all that is in the world, the lust of the flesh and the lust of the eyes and the boastful pride of life, is not from the Father, but is from the world.

The end result of living beyond your means

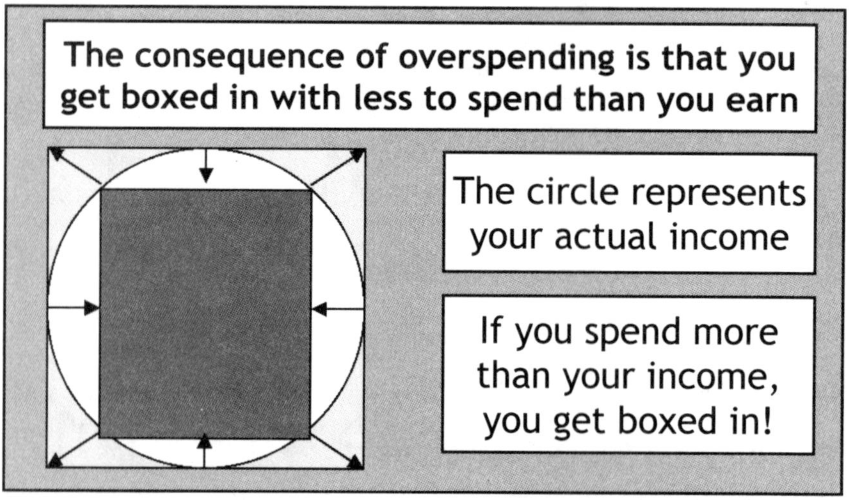

Which of the needs in your life are really wants or desires? What can you do to be more content?

____

____

____

____

____

____

____

Take action!

Step 1

Make a commitment to live within your means.

Proverbs 16:3 (NLT)

[3]Commit your work to the LORD, and then your plans will succeed.

Step 2

Make a plan to live within your means and ask *God* to help.

Proverbs 16:9 (TLB)—see also NASB

[9]We should make plans—counting on God to direct us.

Step 3

Ask God to let you know His plan for you.

Proverbs 20:5 (NKJV)

[5]Counsel in the heart of man is like deep water, But a man of understanding will draw it out.

Why is it hard to live within your means? What steps can you take to stop living beyond your means?

____

____

____

____

____

____

____

____

How to deal with an out-of-balance budget

What is a budget? A budget is a guideline.

Historic-based budgeting

We review all our past expenditures to determine the amount and type of expenditure required to continue to operate the household. History serves as a guideline for the future. For example, when budgeting for clothing, we can estimate how much we will need based on how much we have spent in the past, adjusted by inflation.

Zero-based budgeting

Without regarding our past expenditures, we determine what we are willing to spend for each category to operate the household. This may require us to change our spending habits, or our standard of living. For example, we determine how much we want to spend on each category, within our spending limits. Then we make whatever changes in lifestyle that are necessary, even if it means moving, to live within that budget. This approach does not justify the present or future by the past. Just because we have always done it one way does not mean that it is in the best interest of our family/household goals.

Spending priorities

First part

Belongs to God (tithe)

Malachi 3:8 (NASB)

[8]Will a man rob God? Yet you are robbing Me! But you say, "How have we robbed You?" In tithes and offerings.

Second part

Belongs to the government (taxes)

Matthew 22:21(b) (NLT)

Well, then, He said, give to Caesar what belongs to him. But everything that belongs to God must be given to God.

Third part

Is to meet your needs

1 Timothy 5:8 (NASB)

[8]But if anyone does not provide for his own, and especially for those of his household, he has denied the faith and is worse than an unbeliever.

Fourth part

Is to pay your debts

Psalm 37:21 (TLB)—see also NASB

[21]Evil men borrow and "cannot pay it back"! But the good man returns what he owes with some extra besides.

Fifth part

Is to save/invest

Proverbs 21:20 (NLT)

[20]The wise have wealth and luxury, but fools spend whatever they get.

Problems you can expect to encounter when developing a long-range family plan:

- *Getting all members of the family to participate in the planning.* Plans must not be made by some members and forced upon the others. Confusion, resentment, and even defiance will be the result.
- *Satan will come against you to tell you that planning does not work.* Your thinking might be that planning is a waste of time. Instead, you should focus on your current problems first and deal with them. Satan does not want you to plan. Commit your plans to the Lord, and become stable in your ways because then he loses ground.
- *The husband's ego and pride can be a real problem to planning.* Some men feel threatened by having to surrender their perceived superior position of control and dominance. Men often hide their own insecurities and vulnerabilities from their families.

To combat these and other problems, we must humble ourselves before our God and make a commitment to develop a family or household plan.

2 Chronicles 7:14 (NLT)

[14]Then if My people who are called by My name will humble themselves and pray and seek My face and turn from their wicked ways, I will hear from heaven and will forgive their sins and heal their land.

James 4:6 (NASB)

[6]But He gives a greater grace. Therefore it says, "God is opposed to the proud, but gives grace to the humble."

How does your family system operate:
Do you work as a team?
What can you do to bring the team to cooperation?

____

____

____

____

____

____

____

____

Romans 12:1-3 (NASB)

*[1]Therefore I urge you, brethren, by the mercies of God, to present
your bodies a living and holy sacrifice, acceptable to God, which
is your spiritual service of worship. [2]And do not be conformed
to this world, but be transformed by the renewing of your mind,
so that you may prove what the will of God is, that which is
good and acceptable and perfect. [3]For through the grace given
to me I say to everyone among you not to think more highly of
himself than he ought to think; but to think so as to have sound
judgment, as God has allotted to each a measure of faith.*

1 Peter 5:6-7 (TLB)—see also NASB

*[6]If you will humble yourselves under the mighty hand of God, in
His good time He will lift you up.[7]Let Him have all your worries
and cares, for He is always thinking about you and watching
everything that concerns you.*

Accept God's assurance of His presence in your life!

Deuteronomy 31:6 (TLB)—see also NASB

6Be strong! Be courageous! Do not be afraid of them! For the Lord your God will be with you. He will neither fail you nor forsake you.

Isaiah 42:6 (NLT)

6I, the LORD, have called you to demonstrate My righteousness. I will guard and support you, for I have given you to My people as the personal confirmation of My covenant with them. And you will be a light to guide all nations to Me.

Psalm 91:14-16 (TLB)—see also NASB

14For the Lord says, "Because he loves Me, I will rescue him; I will make him great because he trusts in My Name. 15When he calls on Me, I will answer; I will be with him in trouble and rescue him and honor him. 16I will satisfy him with a full life and give him My salvation."

You can work as a *team*—remember: a house divided against itself will not stand (Matt. 12:25). But a house united cannot fail.

What is your initial plan?

____

____

____

____

____

____

____

What is the first step?

What obstacles do you foresee?

Chapter synthesis

In this chapter we learned that it is possible for us to change our ways. We need to have a plan and *take courage and remember that we can do all things through Christ who strengthens us.* Greater is He who is in us, than is he who is in the world. When we become anxious we find peace and consolation in His Word.

Notes and reflections...

Chapter 12: Building the Foundation

In This Chapter

- Building the foundation
- What you must believe after you are saved
- The Holy Spirit is your helper
- Living the abundant life

In this chapter we will review the key scriptures that tell us that financial freedom is ours. It belongs to us but we must choose it. We must allow God's Word to transform us into the image of His Son. We learned in previous chapters that transformation is a process. We can build a solid and lasting foundation by building our faith in God's Word. Then when the storms of life come, our foundation is solid and will not be moved or washed away.

We are children of God. We have been set free. The Holy Spirit is our helper. We can do all things through Christ who gives us strength.

Financial Freedom is for you!!

Galatians 5:1 (NASB)

It was for freedom that Christ set us free; therefore keep standing firm and do not be subject again to a yoke of slavery.

2 Corinthians 3:17 (NASB)

Now the Lord is the Spirit; and where the Spirit of the Lord is, there is liberty (freedom).

You must choose life!

Deuteronomy 30:15 (NASB)

See, I have set before you today life and prosperity, and death and adversity.

Deuteronomy 30:8-9 (NASB)

Obey the Lord and observe His commandments...then the Lord your God will prosper you abundantly in all the work of your hand...

Be transformed

Romans 12:2 (NASB)

And do not be conformed to this world, but be transformed by the renewing of your mind, so that you may prove what the will of God is, that which is good and acceptable and perfect.

Transformation is a process!

- Psalm 40:4a (NASB): *How blessed is the man who has made the Lord his trust.*
- Trust is unwavering *Faith*
- Faith comes by hearing the Word of God
- The Word of God is truth

Read, *hear*, *speak* the Word and faith will grow until it is unwavering. Then you will be able to truly trust God.

1 Corinthians 1:18 (NASB) For the Word…is the power of God.

The Process of building the foundation

Matthew 21:21-22 (NASB)

[21]And Jesus answered and said to them, "Truly I say to you, if you have faith and do not doubt, you will not only do what was done to the fig tree, but even if you say to this mountain, 'Be taken up and cast into the sea,' it will happen. [22]And all things you ask in prayer, believing, you will receive."

Hebrews 11:6 (NASB)

[6]And without faith it is impossible to please Him, for he who comes to God must believe that He is and that He is a rewarder of those who seek Him.

Hebrews 4:12 (NKJV)

[12]For the Word of God is living and powerful, and sharper than any two-edged sword, piercing even to the division of soul and spirit, and of joints and marrow, and is a discerner of the thoughts and intents of the heart.

Conflict of two natures

Romans 7:14 (NASB)

[14]For we know that the Law is spiritual, but I am of flesh, sold into bondage to sin.

Romans 7:19-20 (NASB)

[19]For the good that I want, I do not do, but I practice the very evil that I do not want. [20]But if I am doing the very thing I do not want, I am no longer the one doing it, but sin which dwells in me.

Galatians 5:17 (NLT)

[17]The old sinful nature loves to do evil, which is just opposite from what the Holy Spirit wants. And the Spirit gives us desires that are opposite from what the sinful nature desires. These two

forces are constantly fighting each other, and your choices are never free from this conflict.

You have been justified by faith!

Romans 5:1-2 (NASB)

[1]Therefore, having been justified by faith, we have peace with God through our Lord Jesus Christ, [2]through whom also we have obtained our introduction by faith into this grace in which we stand; and we exult in hope of the glory of God.

Romans 3:24 (NLT)

[24]Yet now God in His gracious kindness declares us not guilty. He has done this through Christ Jesus, who has freed us by taking away our sins.

Acts 16:31 (NKJV)

[31]So they said, "Believe on the Lord Jesus Christ, and you will be saved, you and your household."

What must you believe after you are saved?

Trust the Word of God is *true*

Matthew 4:4 (NKJV)

[4]But He answered and said, "It is written, 'Man shall not live by bread alone, but by every word that proceeds from the mouth of God.'"

Romans 1:16 (NASB)

[16]For I am not ashamed of the gospel of Christ, for it is the power of God for salvation to everyone who believes, to the Jew first and also to the Greek.

You have been delivered from bondage!

1 John 5:1 (NKJV)

[1]Whoever believes that Jesus is the Christ is born of God, and

everyone who loves Him who begot also loves him who is begotten of Him.

Romans 8:1-2 (NKJV)

[1]There is therefore now no condemnation to those who are in Christ Jesus, who do not walk according to the flesh, but according to the Spirit. [2]For the law of the Spirit of life in Christ Jesus has made me free from the law of sin and death.

Romans 8:5-9 (NASB)

[5]For those who are according to the flesh set their minds on the things of the flesh, but those who are according to the Spirit, the things of the Spirit. [6]For the mind set on the flesh is death, but the mind set on the Spirit is life and peace, [7]because the mind set on the flesh is hostile toward God; for it does not subject itself to the law of God, for it is not even able to do so, [8]and those who are in the flesh cannot please God. [9]However, you are not in the flesh but in the Spirit, if indeed the Spirit of God dwells in you. But if anyone does not have the Spirit of Christ, he does not belong to Him.

You have been set free!

Galatians 5:1 (NKJV)

[1]Stand fast therefore in the liberty by which Christ has made us free, and do not be entangled again with a yoke of bondage.

2 Corinthians 5:17 (NLT)

[17]What this means is that those who become Christians become new persons. They are not the same anymore, for the old life is gone. A new life has begun!

Isaiah 43:18-19 (NASB)

[18]Do not call to mind the former things, Or ponder things of the past. [19]Behold, I will do something new, Now it will spring forth; Will you not be aware of it? I will even make a roadway in the wilderness, Rivers in the desert.

You are God's child

Galatians 3:25-29 (TLB)—see also NASB

[25]But now that Christ has come, we don't need those laws any longer to guard us and lead us to him. [26]For now we are all children of God through faith in Jesus Christ, [27]and we who have been baptized into union with Christ are enveloped by him. [28]We are no longer Jews or Greeks or slaves or free men or even merely men or women, but we are all the same—we are Christians; we are one in Christ Jesus. [29]And now that we are Christ's we are the true descendants of Abraham, and all of God's promises to him belong to us.

Romans 8:14, 16-17 (NASB)

[14]For all who are being led by the Spirit of God, these are sons of God. [16]The Spirit Himself testifies with our spirit that we are children of God, [17]and if children, heirs also, heirs of God and fellow heirs with Christ, if indeed we suffer with Him so that we may also be glorified with Him.

Galatians 4:5-7 (NLT)

[5]God sent Him to buy freedom for us who were slaves to the law, so that He could adopt us as His very own children. [6]And because you Gentiles have become His children, God has sent the Spirit of His Son into your hearts, and now you can call God your dear Father. [7]Now you are no longer a slave but God's own child. And since you are His child, everything He has belongs to you.

The Holy Spirit is your helper

John 14:16-17 (NASB)

[16]I will ask the Father, and He will give you another Helper, that He may be with you forever; [17]that is the Spirit of truth, whom the world cannot receive, because it does not see Him or know Him, but you know Him because He abides with you and will be in you.

John 14:26 (NASB)

[26]But the Helper, the Holy Spirit, whom the Father will send in My name, He will teach you all things, and bring to your remembrance all that I said to you.

Ezekiel 36:26-27 (NASB)

[26]Moreover, I will give you a new heart and put a new spirit
within you; and I will remove the heart of stone from your flesh
and give you a heart of flesh. [27]I will put My Spirit within you
and cause you to walk in My statutes, and you will be careful to
observe My ordinances.

Living the abundant life—is to live in Christ

Galatians 5:16, 17, 25 (NASB)

[16]But I say, walk by the Spirit, and you will not carry out the
desire of the flesh. [17]For the flesh sets its desire against the Spirit,
and the Spirit against the flesh; for these are in opposition to
one another, so that you may not do the things that you please.
[25]If we live by the Spirit, let us also walk by the Spirit.

Romans 8:5-7 (NLT)

[5]Those who are dominated by the sinful nature think about
sinful things, but those who are controlled by the Holy Spirit
think about things that please the Spirit. [6]If your sinful nature
controls your mind, there is death. But if the Holy Spirit controls
your mind, there is life and peace. [7]For the sinful nature is
always hostile to God. It never did obey God's laws, and it never
will.

You cannot serve God and please men

Galatians 1:10 (NASB)

[10]For am I now seeking the favor of men, or of God? Or am I striving to please men? If I were still trying to please men, I would not be a bond-servant of Christ.

Psalm 51:10-12 (NASB)

10Create in me a clean heart, O God, And renew a steadfast spirit within me. 11Do not cast me away from Your presence And do not take Your Holy Spirit from me. 12Restore to me the joy of Your salvation And sustain me with a willing spirit.

Psalm 55:22 (NASB)

22Cast your burden upon the LORD and He will sustain you; He will never allow the righteous to be shaken.

Chapter synthesis

When temptation and trials come—when the battle for freedom rages—seek comfort in His Word

Whenever you are confronted with a trial, do not be consumed by the problems. First read from His Word to find comfort. You will not be able to read the entire group of verses without experiencing the peace of God in your life. Then go deal with the problem!

Notes and reflections…

Appendix: Daily Reflection—Seek Comfort from His Word

In This Appendix

- Bible verses for reflection and comfort

Over the years, as I went through the transformation process, I became discouraged and worried from time to time. Sometimes the struggles seemed more than I could handle. It was through those difficult periods that I found the following scriptures that would comfort me and encourage me to continue.

I can say without a shadow of a doubt that whenever I am confronted with a situation or problem, I can find peace in the scriptures. If and when you are confronted with struggles in your life, read these scriptures and I promise you that you will be at peace before you get to the end. God's Word is healing not only to your body but also to your soul.

When the battle for freedom rages, seek comfort in His Word

Psalm 138:7-8 (NASB)

7 Though I walk in the midst of trouble, You will revive me; You will stretch forth Your hand against the wrath of my enemies, And Your right hand will save me.

8 The LORD will accomplish what concerns me; Your lovingkindness, O LORD, is everlasting; Do not forsake the works of Your hands.

Proverbs 3:5-6 (NKJV)

5 Trust in the LORD with all your heart, And lean not on your own understanding; 6 In all your ways acknowledge Him, And He shall direct your paths.

Proverbs 3:25-26 (NASB)

25 Do not be afraid of sudden fear Nor of the onslaught of the wicked when it comes; 26 For the LORD will be your confidence And will keep your foot from being caught.

Exodus 23:20-33 (NASB)

20 Behold, I am going to send an angel before you to guard you along the way and to bring you into the place which I have prepared. 21 Be on your guard before him and obey his voice; do not be rebellious toward him, for he will not pardon your transgression, since My name is in him. 22 But if you truly obey his voice and do all that I say, then I will be an enemy to your enemies and an adversary to your adversaries. 23 For My angel will go before you and bring you in to the land of the Amorites, the Hittites, the Perizzites, the Canaanites, the Hivites and the Jebusites; and I will completely destroy them. 24 You shall not worship their gods, nor serve them, nor do according to their deeds; but you shall utterly overthrow them and break their sacred pillars in pieces. 25 But you shall serve the LORD your God, and He will bless your bread and your water; and I will remove sickness from your midst. 26 There shall be no one miscarrying or barren in your land; I will fulfill the number of your days. 27 I will send My terror ahead of you, and throw

into confusion all the people among whom you come, and I will
make all your enemies turn their backs to you. [28]I will send
hornets ahead of you so that they will drive out the Hivites, the
Canaanites, and the Hittites before you. [29]I will not drive them
out before you in a single year, that the land may not become
desolate and the beasts of the field become too numerous for
you. [30]I will drive them out before you little by little, until you
become fruitful and take possession of the land. [31]I will fix your
boundary from the Red Sea to the sea of the Philistines, and
from the wilderness to the River Euphrates; for I will deliver
the inhabitants of the land into your hand, and you will drive
them out before you. [32]You shall make no covenant with them or
with their gods. [33]They shall not live in your land, because they
will make you sin against Me; for if you serve their gods, it will
surely be a snare to you.

Deuteronomy 31:6, 8 (NASB)

[6]Be strong and courageous, do not be afraid or tremble at them,
for the LORD your God is the one who goes with you. He will not
fail you or forsake you. [8]The LORD is the one who goes ahead of
you; He will be with you. He will not fail you or forsake you. Do
not fear or be dismayed.

Isaiah 40:31 (NKJV)

[31]But those who wait on the LORD Shall renew their strength;
They shall mount up with wings like eagles, They shall run and
not be weary, They shall walk and not faint.

Isaiah 41:8-10 (NLT)

[8]But as for you, Israel My servant, Jacob My chosen one,
descended from My friend Abraham, [9]I have called you back
from the ends of the earth so you can serve Me. For I have chosen
you and will not throw you away. [10]Don't be afraid, for I am with
you. Do not be dismayed, for I am your God. I will strengthen
you. I will help you. I will uphold you with My victorious right
hand.

Isaiah 42:6-9 (NLT)

[6]I, the LORD, have called you to demonstrate My righteousness.
I will guard and support you, for I have given you to My people
as the personal confirmation of My covenant with them. And

you will be a light to guide all nations to Me. [7]You will open the eyes of the blind and free the captives from prison. You will release those who sit in dark dungeons.

[8]I am the LORD; that is My Name! I will not give My glory to anyone else. I will not share My praise with carved idols. [9]Everything I prophesied has come true, and now I will prophesy again. I will tell you the future before it happens.

Isaiah 43:1-3 (NLT)

[1]But now, O Israel, the LORD who created you says: "Do not be afraid, for I have ransomed you. I have called you by name; you are Mine. [2]When you go through deep waters and great trouble, I will be with you. When you go through rivers of difficulty, you will not drown! When you walk through the fire of oppression, you will not be burned up; the flames will not consume you. [3]For I am the LORD, your God, the Holy One of Israel, your Savior. I gave Egypt, Ethiopia, and Seba as a ransom for your freedom."

Matthew 11:28-30 (NASB)

[28]Come to Me, all who are weary and heavy-laden, and I will give you rest. [29]Take My yoke upon you and learn from Me, for I am gentle and humble in heart, and you will find rest for your souls.. [30]For My yoke is easy and My burden is light.

John 8:36 (NKJV)

[36]Therefore if the Son makes you free, you shall be free indeed.

John 15:1-6 (NASB)

[1]I am the true vine, and My Father is the vinedresser. [2]Every branch in Me that does not bear fruit, He takes away; and every branch that bears fruit, He prunes it so that it may bear more fruit. [3]You are already clean because of the word which I have spoken to you. [4]Abide in Me, and I in you. As the branch cannot bear fruit of itself unless it abides in the vine, so neither can you unless you abide in Me. [5]I am the vine, you are the branches; he who abides in Me and I in him, he bears much fruit, for apart from Me you can do nothing. [6]If anyone does not abide in Me, he is thrown away as a branch and dries up; and they gather them, and cast them into the fire and they are burned.

Romans 8:28-31 (NASB)

[28]And we know that God causes all things to work together for good to those who love God, to those who are called according to His purpose. [29]For those whom He foreknew, He also predestined to become conformed to the image of His Son, so that He would be the firstborn among many brethren; [30]and these whom He predestined, He also called; and these whom He called, He also justified; and these whom He justified, He also glorified.

[31]What then shall we say to these things? If God is for us, who is against us?

1 Corinthians 9:19 (NKJV)

[19]For though I am free from all men, I have made myself a servant to all, that I might win the more...

2 Corinthians 4:8-18 (NLT)

[8]We are pressed on every side by troubles, but we are not crushed and broken. We are perplexed, but we don't give up and quit. [9]We are hunted down, but God never abandons us. We get knocked down, but we get up again and keep going. [10]Through suffering, these bodies of ours constantly share in the death of Jesus so that the life of Jesus may also be seen in our bodies.

[11]Yes, we live under constant danger of death because we serve Jesus, so that the life of Jesus will be obvious in our dying bodies. [12]So we live in the face of death, but it has resulted in eternal life for you.

[13]But we continue to preach because we have the same kind of faith the psalmist had when he said, "I believed in God, and so I speak." [14]We know that the same God who raised our Lord Jesus will also raise us with Jesus and present us to himself along with you. [15]All of these things are for your benefit. And as God's grace brings more and more people to Christ, there will be great thanksgiving, and God will receive more and more glory.

[16]That is why we never give up. Though our bodies are dying, our spirits are being renewed every day. [17]For our present troubles are quite small and won't last very long. Yet they produce for us an immeasurably great glory that will last forever! [18]So we don't look at the troubles we can see right now; rather, we look

forward to what we have not yet seen. For the troubles we see will soon be over, but the joys to come will last forever.

Ephesians 6:10-18 (NASB)

10 Finally, be strong in the Lord and in the strength of His might. 11 Put on the full armor of God, so that you will be able to stand firm against the schemes of the devil. 12 For our struggle is not against flesh and blood, but against the rulers, against the powers, against the world forces of this darkness, against the spiritual forces of wickedness in the heavenly places. 13 Therefore, <u>take up the full armor of God</u>, so that you will be able to resist in the evil day, and having done everything, to stand firm. 14 Stand firm therefore, HAVING GIRDED YOUR LOINS WITH TRUTH, *and* HAVING PUT ON THE BREASTPLATE OF RIGHTEOUSNESS, *15 and having shod* YOUR FEET WITH THE PREPARATION OF THE GOSPEL OF PEACE; *16 in addition to all, taking up the shield of faith with which you will be able to extinguish all the flaming arrows of the evil one. 17 And take* THE HELMET OF SALVATION, *and the sword of the Spirit, which is the Word of God.*

18 With all prayer and petition pray at all times in the Spirit, and with this in view, be on the alert with all perseverance and petition for all the saints.

Hebrews 10:35-36 (NASB)

35 Therefore, do not throw away your confidence, which has a great reward. 36 For you have need of endurance, so that when you have done the will of God, you may receive what was promised.

James 1:2-4 (NASB)

2 Consider it all joy, my brethren, when you encounter various trials, 3 knowing that the testing of your faith produces endurance. 4 And let endurance have its perfect result, so that you may be <u>perfect and complete, lacking in nothing</u>.

1 Peter 4:12-13 (NASB)

12 Beloved, do not be surprised at the fiery ordeal among you, which comes upon you for your testing, as though some strange thing were happening to you; 13 but to the degree that you share the sufferings of Christ, keep on rejoicing, so that also at the revelation of His glory you may rejoice with exultation.

1 Peter 5:10 (NASB)

*[10]After you have suffered for a little while, the God of all grace,
who called you to His eternal glory in Christ, will Himself
perfect, confirm, strengthen and establish you.*

Luke 11:1-13 (NASB)

*[1]It happened that while Jesus was praying in a certain place,
after He had finished, one of His disciples said to Him, "Lord,
teach us to pray just as John also taught his disciples." [2]And He
said to them, "When you pray, say:*

Father, hallowed be Your name.

Your kingdom come.

[3]Give us each day our daily bread.

[4]And forgive us our sins,

For we ourselves also forgive everyone who is indebted to us.

And lead us not into temptation."

*[5]Then He said to them, "Suppose one of you has a friend, and
goes to him at midnight and says to him, 'Friend, lend me three
loaves; [6]for a friend of mine has come to me from a journey, and
I have nothing to set before him'; [7]and from inside he answers
and says, 'Do not bother me; the door has already been shut
and my children and I are in bed; I cannot get up and give
you anything.' [8]I tell you, even though he will not get up and
give him anything because he is his friend, yet because of his
persistence he will get up and give him as much as he needs.*

*[9]So I say to you, ask, and it will be given to you; seek, and you
will find; knock, and it will be opened to you. [10]For everyone who
asks, receives; and he who seeks, finds; and to him who knocks,
it will be opened. [11]Now suppose one of you fathers is asked by
his son for a fish; he will not give him a snake instead of a fish,
will he? [12]Or if he is asked for an egg, he will not give him a
scorpion, will he? [13]If you then, being evil, know how to give
good gifts to your children, how much more will your heavenly
Father give the Holy Spirit to those who ask Him?"*

Luke 11:16-17 (NASB)

16 Others, to test Him, were demanding of Him a sign from heaven.
17 But He knew their thoughts and said to them, "Any kingdom divided against itself is laid waste; and a house divided against itself falls."

Other Books in the Abundant Freedom Series

For further information about our Ministry and Publications visit our website:

www.AbundantFreedomMinistries.com

or write to Abundant Freedom Press,

P.O. Box 461316, Aurora, Colorado, 80046